Book 2

Music Theory for the Successful String Musician

A Curriculum of Theory, History, and Creativity
Lessons and Exercises for Well-Rounded String Students

Christopher R. Selby

GIA Publications, Inc.
Chicago

Available Editions:

Book 1

Violin	G-9941
Viola	G-9942
Cello	G-9943
Bass	G-9944

Book 2

Violin	G-10115
Viola	G-10116
Cello	G-10117
Bass	G-10118

Teacher's Edition (Book 1 & 2)	G-9945

Music Theory for the Successful String Musician, Book 2 - Violin
Christopher R. Selby

G-10115
ISBN: 978-1-62277-429-6

7404 S. Mason Avenue, Chicago, IL 60638
www.giamusic.com

Music Theory for the Successful String Musician

Book 2

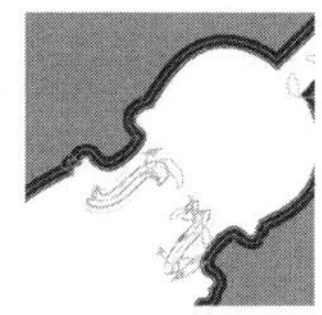

Unit 14. Fingerboard Map Review

LESSON 14.1

Fingerboard Map Review

In Book 1 you learned that a **natural** note is neither sharp nor flat. There are two pairs of natural notes that are separated by a **half step**: B-C and E-F. All other natural notes are separated by a whole step; they have a note between them with a sharp (♯) name and a flat (♭) name. In Exercise 14.1 below, you can see that the space between C and D is occupied by both C♯ and D♭. These **enharmonic** notes have different names and look different on the staff, but they are played the same way and sound the same. The enharmonic spelling for C♯ is D♭, and the enharmonic spelling of D♭ is C♯.

Exercise 14.1. Enharmonic Spelling

1. In each open space on the string diagram below, draw a diagonal line and write both the sharp and flat note name between the natural notes that are separated by a whole step. The space between C and D has been done for you.

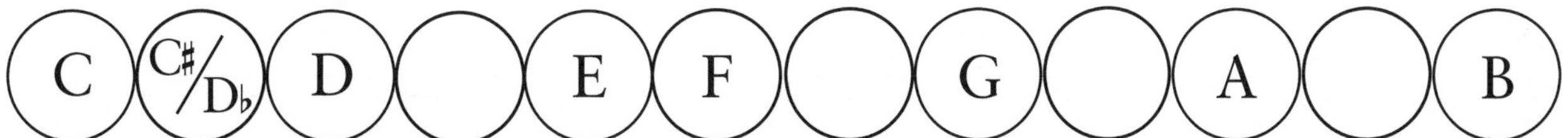

2. Write the enharmonic spelling for each note below.

A♯ = _____ C♯ = _____ D♯ = _____ F♯ = _____ G♯ = _____
A♭ = _____ B♭ = _____ D♭ = _____ E♭ = _____ G♭ = _____

3. Fill in the fingerboard map below. Write the note names of your open strings in the four circles to the left of the line, with the lowest string on the bottom. Fill in all of the natural notes on your instrument. Remember, B-C and E-F are half steps and are in adjacent circles. They should touch because they have no notes between them. Finally, draw diagonal lines in the remaining circles and write the sharp note names on the left side of the diagonal line and flat note names on the right.

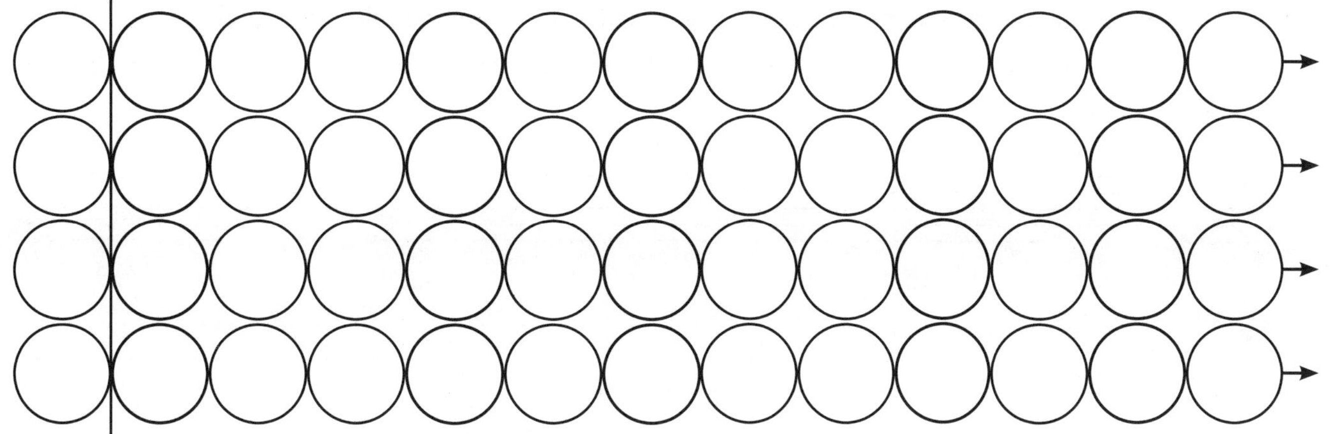

LESSON 14.2

Writing Chromatic Scales

A **chromatic** scale is a scale made up entirely of half steps, like the scales written below. When writing with sharps, the descending scale requires naturals to cancel out the sharps. When writing with flats, the ascending scale requires naturals to cancel the flats. Half step marks (⁄⁀\ ) have been placed over the natural half steps to show that there are no sharp notes between B-C and E-F.

Exercise 14.2. Writing Chromatic Scales

1. Refer to the two chromatic scales in the examples above, and copy them exactly to the two staves below. Include half step marks, and do not add extra notes between B-C and E-F.

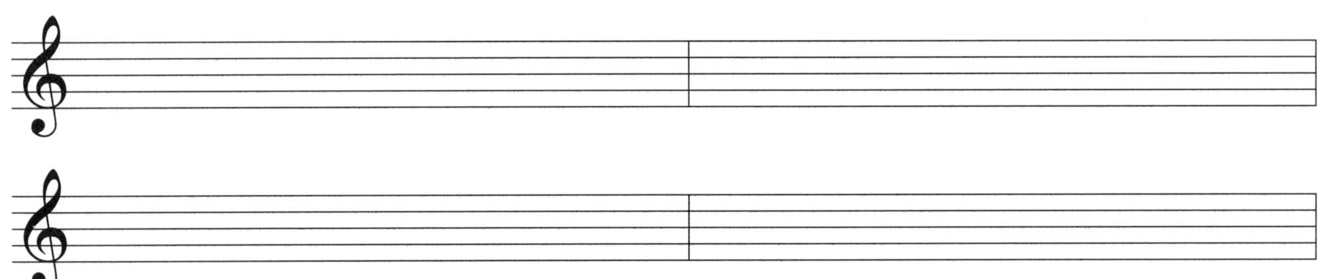

2. *Use sharp and natural accidentals only* to write a two-octave ascending and descending chromatic scale that starts and ends with your lowest open string note. Write half step symbols over the pairs of natural half steps (B-C and E-F).

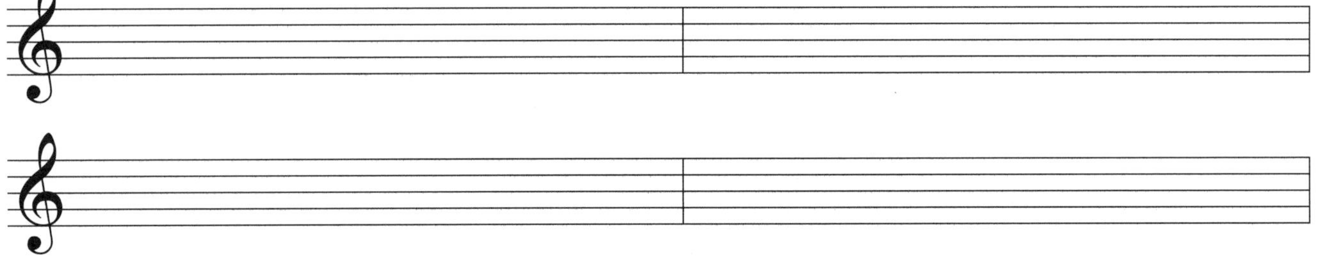

3. *Use flat and natural accidentals only* to write a two-octave ascending and descending chromatic scale that starts and ends with your lowest open string note. Write half step symbols over the pairs of natural half steps (B-C and E-F).

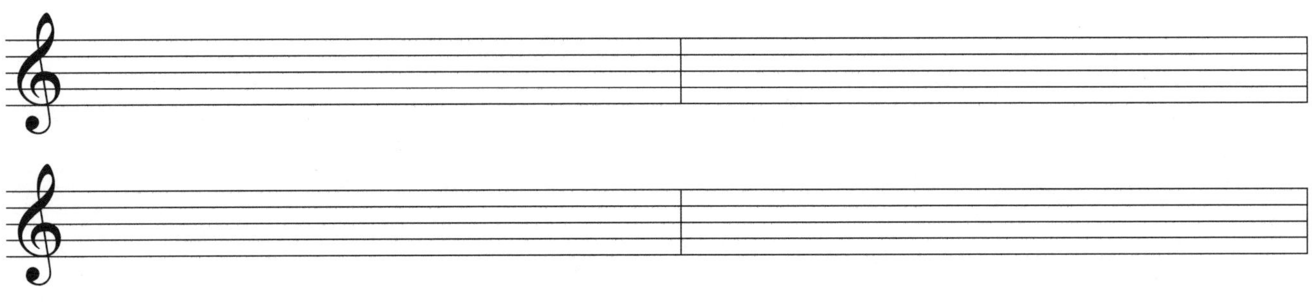

LESSON 14.3

Reviewing Major and Minor Seconds

A **second** is an **interval** with two notes that are next to each other on the staff. When the letter names are adjacent to each other—such as A to B or G to A—then the interval is a second. There are two common types of seconds, as shown in the diagram to the right: **Major** (bigger) seconds are always whole steps, and **minor** (smaller) seconds are always half steps. But be careful: Not all half steps are minor seconds. For example, C to C♯ is *not* a second, but C to D♭ is.

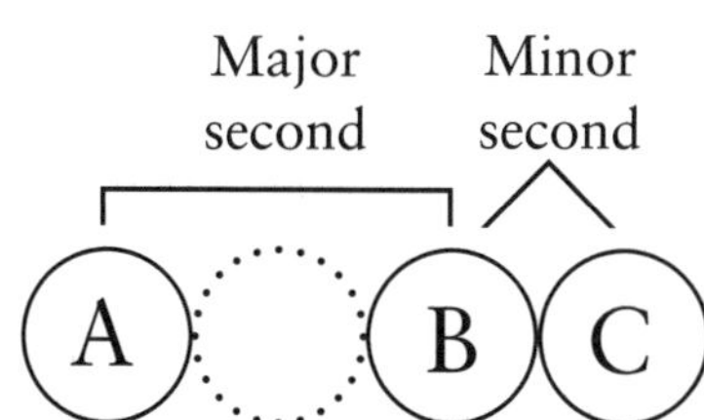

Exercise 14.3. Reviewing Major and Minor Seconds

1. Each measure below has a key signature and four notes. Determine which notes are natural, sharp, or flat, and write the names of the four notes in the correct spaces on the fingerboard diagram below the staff. Shade in the remaining spaces on the fingerboard that represent other notes not on the staff. The first one has been done for you.

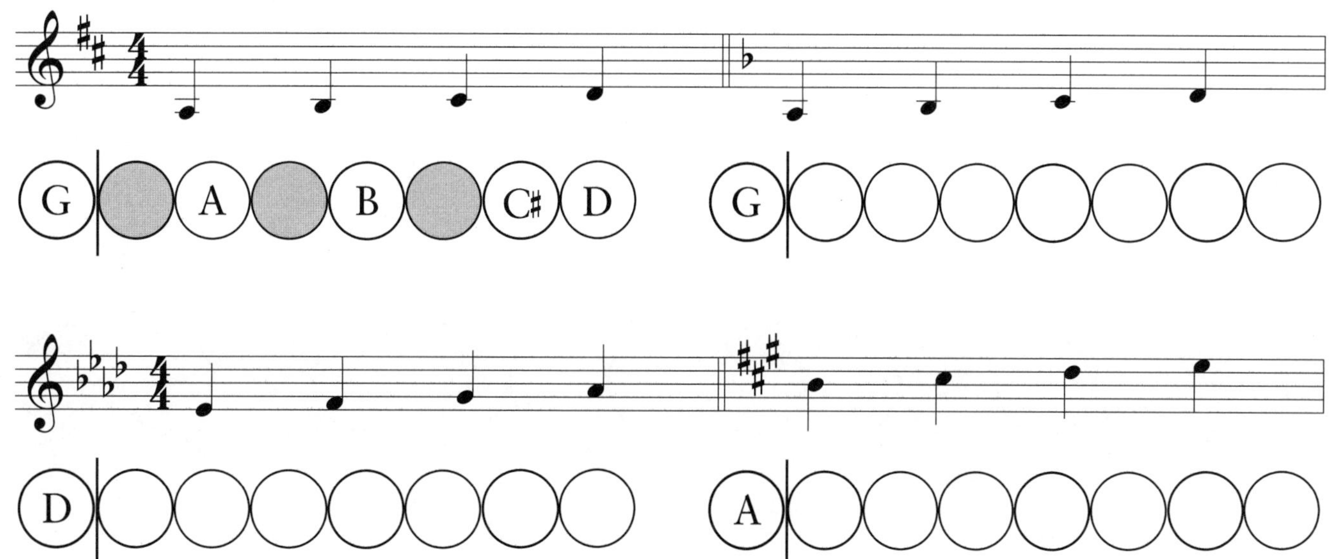

In the next exercises, write the notehead first and then figure out if you need an accidental to make the interval minor or major. The first measure in each line has been done as an example.

2. Write the note that is a *minor second higher* than the given note, as shown in the first measure.

3. Write the note that is a *minor second lower* than the given note, as shown in the first measure.

Exercise 14.3. Reviewing Major and Minor Seconds (cont.)

4. Write the note that is a *major second higher* than the given note, as shown in the first measure.

5. Write the note that is a *major second lower* than the given note, as shown in the first measure.

6. On the fingerboard map below, write the names of your open strings in the circles to the left of the line, starting with the highest string in the top circle. Then:
   - Look at the key signature to the right and fill in all of the sharp *and* natural notes in that key. Each string will look like a scale with half steps and whole steps.
   - Shade in the remaining spaces on the fingerboard that represent other notes not in that key signature. The lowest string has been done for you.

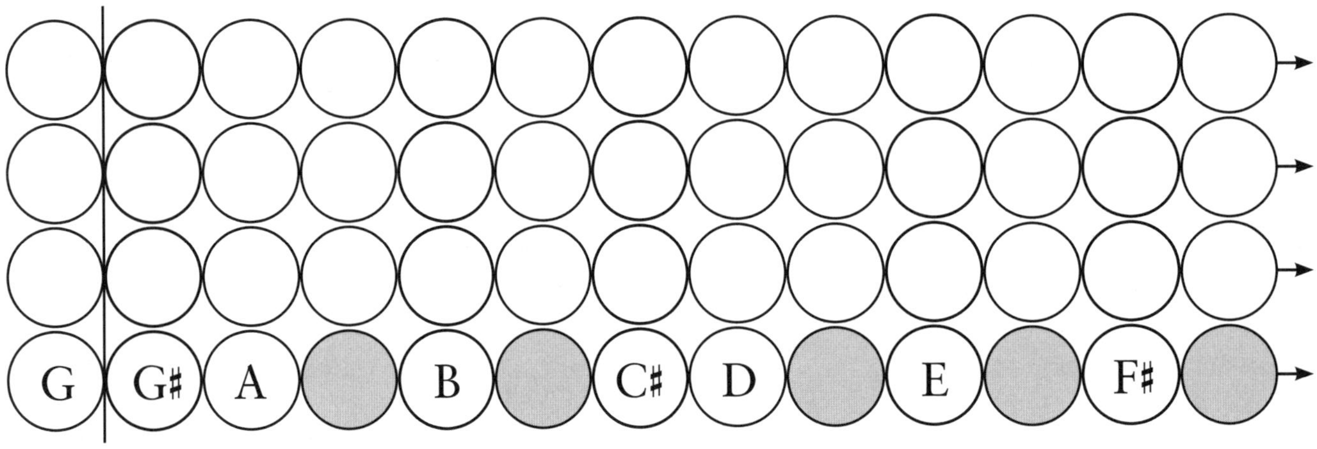

Unit 14 Study Guide

On a separate piece of paper, answer the following questions:

1. Explain the difference between a sharp, flat, and natural note. Explain the term *enharmonic*.
2. What is the enharmonic spelling for A♯, C♯, D♯, F♯, G♯, A♭, B♭, D♭, E♭, and G♭?
3. Complete a chromatic fingerboard map without help.
4. What two pairs of natural notes are separated by a half step? What is a chromatic scale?
5. On staff paper, write a two-octave ascending and descending chromatic scale using only sharps and naturals. Then write a two-octave ascending and descending chromatic scale using only flats and naturals.
6. What is a minor second? What is a major second?
7. What notes are a minor second above A, B, C, D, E, F, and G? What notes are a major second above?
8. What notes are a minor second below A, B, C, D, E, F, and G? What notes are a major second below?
9. Use a blank fingerboard map to fill in the names of the notes that belong to the key signature of one of your concert pieces (as you did in Question 6 of Exercise 14.3).

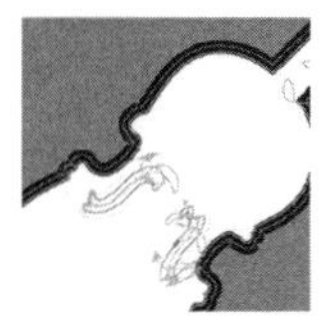

Unit 15. Simple Meter with Sixteenth Notes

LESSON 15.1

Simple Meter Review

In Book 1 you learned that we use the term **meter** to identify how beats in music are grouped and divided. Meters with beats organized into groups of two are called **duple meter**, and they usually have **time signatures** with even top numbers like $\frac{2}{4}$ and $\frac{4}{4}$. Meters with three beats in a group are called **triple meter** and have time signatures like $\frac{3}{4}$.

In simple meters, the upper number generally tells us how many beats are in a measure.

The lower number tells us what note value gets the beat. The 4 on the bottom means the quarter note gets the beat.

C is a time signature called common time, which is the same as $\frac{4}{4}$ and has four quarter notes per measure.

$\frac{2}{4}$ = 2/♩ = 2 ♩ beats per measure

$\frac{3}{4}$ = 3/♩ = 3 ♩ beats per measure

$\frac{4}{4}$ = 4/♩ = 4 ♩ beats per measure

C = 4/♩ = 4 ♩ beats per measure

Exercise 15.1. Simple Meter Review

1. In each measure below, write the correct number of quarter notes to illustrate the time signature.

$\frac{3}{4}$ | $\frac{4}{4}$ | $\frac{2}{4}$ | C | $\frac{5}{4}$ |

2. In the space at the beginning of each measure below, write the time signature associated with the rhythm in that measure.

3. In the first measure below, we have written quarter note stems above each beat. There are four stems (beats) in each measure of $\frac{4}{4}$. Half notes and half rests get two evenly spaced stem/beat marks, and whole notes and whole rests get four. Write stems over each beat in the remaining measures, and write the beat numbers over each stem to complete the exercise.

Exercise 15.1. Simple Meter Review (cont.)

4. How many eighth notes go in a quarter note? _____ Half note? _____Whole note? _____
5. Follow the steps below to write eighth note stems, beams, and beat numbers.
   - Step 1: Write eighth note stems over the notes in the last two measures of the exercise below.
   - Step 2: Add beams to each pair of eighth note stems.
   - Step 3: Write the beat numbers over the first eighth note in each pair, as shown in the first two measures.
   - Step 4: Then perform the rhythm with your bow hand while counting out the eighth notes.

1 2 3 4 1 2 3 4

6. Over the music below, write eighth note stems, beams, and beat numbers like you did in Question 5. Remember to carefully space the correct number of stems over the longer notes and rests. Then perform the rhythm with your bow hand while counting out the eighth notes.

7. The music below is in a different meter. There should be six stems and three beams per measure. Write eighth note stems, add beams, and write the beat numbers over the first eighth note of each pair. Then perform the rhythm with your bow hand while counting out the eighth notes.

LESSON 15.2

Sixteenth Note Rhythms in Simple Meter

One quarter note equals four sixteenth notes, and one eighth note equals two sixteenths. A single sixteenth note (𝅘𝅥𝅯) has two flags on the right side of the stem, and a sixteenth rest (𝄿) is like an eighth rest with two flags. Multiple sixteenths are connected with a double beam and are usually grouped in fours, as shown to the right.

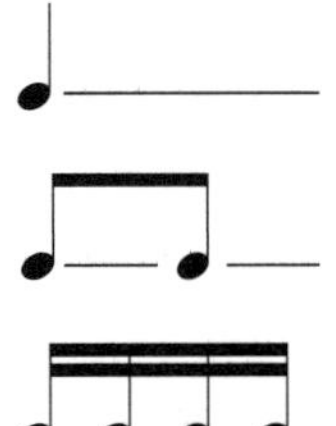

When counting sixteenth note rhythms, use your teacher's counting system or the traditional system: 1 e + a, 2 e + a, 3 e + a, 4 e + a. The syllables are easier to pronounce if the "d" is pronounced with the last "a": 1-e-an-da, 2-e-an-da, 3-e-an-da, 4-e-an-da.

Exercise 15.2. Sixteenth Note Rhythms in Simple Meter

1. In the musical example below, how many sixteenth note stems are written over each eighth note? _____ How many are over each quarter note? _____ Half note? _____ Dotted quarter note? _____

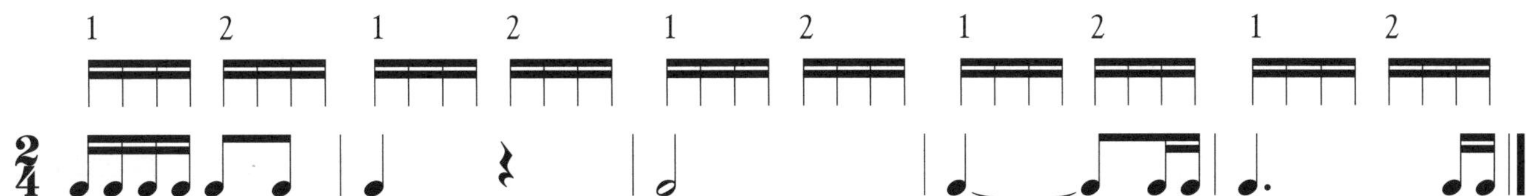

2. Refer to the music example above to help you write sixteenth note stems, beams, and beat numbers over the new music example below. In $\frac{2}{4}$ there should be two beats (two groups of four sixteenth note stems) in each measure.
   - Step 1: Write the correct number of sixteenth note stems over each note. The first stem goes over the note itself, and any remaining stems should be spaced evenly before the next note or rest.
   - Step 2: Add double beams to each group of four sixteenth note stems.
   - Step 3: Write the beat numbers over the first sixteenth note of each beamed group as shown above.

3. Write sixteenth note stems, beams, and beat numbers over the example below. It is in $\frac{3}{4}$, so it will have three beats (three groups of four sixteenth note stems) in each measure.

4. Write sixteenth note stems, beams, and beat numbers over the example below. It is in $\frac{4}{4}$, so it will have four beats (four groups of four sixteenth note stems) in each measure.

5. IMPORTANT: Perform the rhythms written above with your bow hand while counting (1 e + a, 2 e + a, etc.) in a steady tempo.

LESSON 15.3

Sixteenth Note Syncopation and Dotted Rhythms

The dot in a **dotted rhythm** increases the length of a note by half its value. So if a normal eighth note or eighth rest is as long as two sixteenths, then a dotted eighth note or rest is as long as three sixteenths, as shown below on the left. Therefore, three sixteenth note stems should be marked over dotted eighth notes and rests, also shown below.

The rhythms in the next section include dots, ties, and **syncopation**. They are relatively easy to mark but more difficult to count and perform. After you write sixteenth note stems, beams, and beat numbers over the music, practice counting (1 e + a, 2 e + a) while performing the rhythms with your bow hand.

Exercise 15.3. Sixteenth Note Syncopation and Dotted Rhythms

1. In the first measure below, how many sixteenth note stems go into the dotted eighth? _____ Over the remaining measures, write sixteenth note stems, double beam the stems in groups of four, and write the beat numbers over each beam. Check your work: There should be two beats (two groups of four sixteenth note stems) in each measure. Longer notes and rests should have the correct number of evenly spaced stems.

2. In the first measure below, how many sixteenth stems go into the syncopated eighth note in beat 2? _____ Over the remaining measures, write sixteenth note stems, beams, and beat numbers. This music is in $\frac{3}{4}$, so it should have three beats (three groups of four sixteenth note stems) in each measure.

3. Sixteenth rests disrupt the beams that help us see the beats. Carefully write the correct number of sixteenth stems over each note. HINT: Write and count all of the stems before grouping them with beams.

4. Remember to perform all of the rhythm exercises on this page with your bow hand while counting (1 e + a, 2 e + a) with a steady pulse. Can you perform these challenging rhythms without help?

LESSON 15.4

Subdividing with Sixteenth Notes

Counting sixteenth notes through longer notes and rests is called "subdividing." Professional musicians subdivide in order to read challenging dotted and syncopated rhythms correctly. It is especially important to subdivide during the long notes and rests. Count and perform the rhythm below. The arrows will help you identify beats that begin in the middle of the notes.

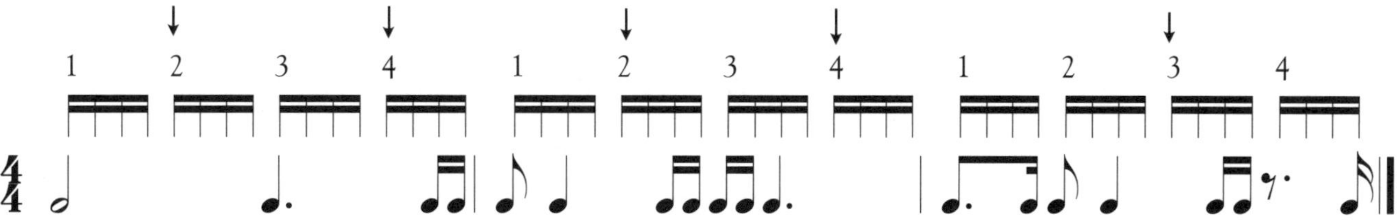

Exercise 15.4. Subdividing with Sixteenth Notes

1. In the first measure below, how many sixteenth note stems are in the dotted quarter? _____ Which beats occur in the middle of a long note? ______________________ Over the remaining measures, write sixteenth note stems, beams, and beat numbers. Then perform the rhythm with your bow hand while counting sixteenths.

2. Write sixteenth note stems, beams, and beat numbers over the exercise below. For best results, write all the sixteenth note stems first, and then add beams and beat numbers. Then perform the rhythm while counting.

3. Write all sixteenth note stems first, and then add beams and beat numbers. Then perform the rhythm while counting.

Unit 15 Study Guide

On a separate piece of paper, answer Questions 1–4. For additional practice, try Questions 5 and 6.

1. How is duple meter different from triple meter? Give examples of time signatures for each meter.
2. What do the top and bottom numbers in a simple meter time signature tell us?
3. In a dotted rhythm, how much time does the dot add to the dotted note?
4. What does it mean to "subdivide"? How many sixteenths go into a ♪. ? ♩. ? 𝅗𝅥. ?
5. Count and perform the rhythms in this unit for a stand partner or friend.
6. Find some sight-reading exercises or concert music with challenging sixteenth note rhythms. Then mark the music with sixteenth note stems, beams, and beat numbers, and perform the rhythms while counting.

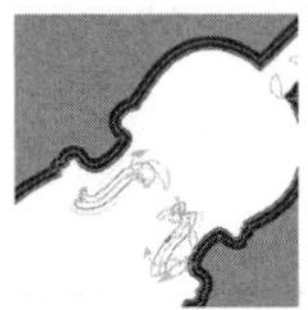

Unit 16. The Baroque Masters

During a time called the **Renaissance era** (1400–1600), the Church was very rich and powerful. As a result, most of the surviving music from the Renaissance era is religious or "sacred" music written for church services, events, or holidays. Most sacred music is vocal music with religious text that is sung by soloists and a choir. This period is called the *Renaissance*—which means "rebirth"—because people like Galileo, Leonardo da Vinci, and many other inventors, artists, and writers began making significant scientific and philosophical advancements that brought the world into the modern era. More people began to question the divine right and power of the Church, and they also began exploring what it means to be human. This cultural shift is reflected in the explosion of "secular" (non-religious) art, literature, and music during the Renaissance and in the years to follow.

In the **Baroque era** (1600–1750) continued scientific advancements led to the creation of new and better musical instruments, which set the stage for new instrumental works like sonatas, concertos, and dance suites. Secular music began to flourish in the homes of the rich nobility as well as in theaters that were built for public plays and concerts. The newest and most popular secular music sweeping across Europe was Baroque opera, written by composers like George Frideric Handel. **Opera** is a play set to music, with dramatic acting, staging, and costumes, and a storyline and text for vocal soloists and chorus. People paid good money to see operas with their favorite soloists, who were like the rock stars and movie stars of their day.

Of course, sacred music was still very common during the Baroque era, and composers like Johann Sebastian Bach wrote many hundreds of sacred cantatas (works that are sung) and oratorios for the Church. An **oratorio** has vocal soloists and a choir that tell a story, often a Biblical story. Unlike opera, however, oratorios have no acting, staging, or costumes.

LESSON 16.1

Johann Sebastian Bach

Johann Sebastian Bach (1685–1750) was a German composer whose ingenious use of harmony served as a model for many of the great composers who followed him. He was a virtuoso organist, and when he was eighteen he graduated from music school and got a job as a church organist and music director. He spent most of his life working for a variety of churches in this roll, composing over three hundred cantatas and hundreds of other sacred works for his church choirs.

Bach wrote a large amount of secular music as well. When he was young, he studied the string works of **Vivaldi** and **Corelli** and rewrote them for harpsichord and organ. He also wrote six **suites** for unaccompanied cello, six **sonatas** and partitas for unaccompanied violin, four orchestral suites, six *Brandenburg Concertos*, and many other concertos, including his famous double concerto for two violins.

Bach had seven children with his first wife, Maria Barbara, and thirteen more with his second wife, Anna Magdalena. Half of his twenty children died before reaching adulthood, a challenging but normal part of life at that time. Being a kid in the 1700s was difficult, but Bach's ten surviving children still found time to study, do chores, and practice their instruments. Several of his sons, including Johann Christian (J. C.) and Carl Philipp Emanuel (C. P. E.), grew up to be respected composers who broke away from the Baroque style and helped establish a new, simpler Classical style.

LESSON 16.2

George Frideric Handel

George Frideric Handel (1685–1759) was born the same year as Bach, and they grew up less than a hundred miles from each other. The two great composers never met, and their lives were very different. Bach was a church musician who remained relatively unknown throughout his life, but Handel was a superstar whose operas and oratorios were known around Europe during his lifetime.

Handel showed enormous talent as a child and was composing by the age of nine. He studied music at the university in his hometown of Halle, Germany. At the age of twenty-seven, Handel settled down in London, where he quickly proved himself to be a brilliant composer with a gift and passion for stage productions. Handel started three commercial opera companies and wrote more than forty operas over thirty years. By the late 1730s, however, the people of London were becoming tired of Baroque opera, so Handel turned to the oratorio to make a living. Handel wrote twenty-nine oratorios in his later life, and by far the most popular of these was *Messiah*, which contains the famous "Hallelujah" chorus. He wrote the entire three-hour work in twenty-four days, and it was such a huge hit when it opened in 1742 that Handel never wrote another opera.

While in London, Handel wrote many instrumental works as well. He wrote violin sonatas and a collection of **concerti grossi** modeled after the very popular works by Corelli. In 1717, he wrote his most famous orchestral work, *Water Music*, for a royal boat party for the King of England, George I. Handel's orchestra played the *Water Music* for hours on a barge alongside the king's boat, and the Londoners came out to listen along the shore of the River Thames. Thirty years later, the king's son, George II, requested *Music for the Royal Fireworks* for another outdoor party that had an audience of twelve thousand. Handel died a wealthy and famous composer in 1759. He was given a state funeral and buried in London's Westminster Abbey.

Exercise 16.1. Short Essay: The Baroque Masters

Select a Baroque composer from the following list: Johann Sebastian Bach, Arcangelo Corelli, George Frideric Handel, Henry Purcell, Georg Telemann, Antonio Vivaldi. Then write a short essay that answers the following questions: When and where did the composer live throughout his life? For whom did the composer write music? (In other words, how did he make a living?) In what forms of composition did this person excel (operas, sonatas, church music, concertos)? And what musical contributions did this composer make to the world of music?

Unit 16 Study Guide

On a separate piece of paper, answer the following questions:

1. What was the *Renaissance*, and why was it called that? Why is most surviving Renaissance music vocal music?
2. What changes in the world led to the creation of instrumental sonatas and concertos during the Baroque era?
3. Explain the difference between sacred and secular music, and list several examples of each.
4. What is an oratorio, and how is it different from opera?
5. Describe the main contributions that Bach and Handel made to the music world.

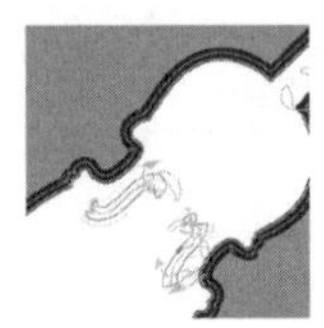

Unit 17. Tetrachords and Thirds

LESSON 17.1

Tetrachord Spelling

A **tetrachord** is a group of four consecutive notes separated by major and minor seconds. Their spellings are always stepwise. They never skip a note name, and they do not repeat a note name, like going from C to C♯.

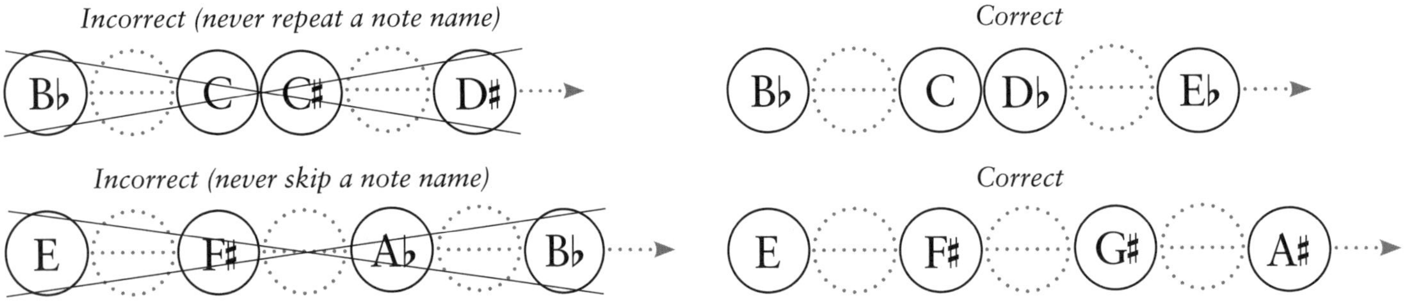

Incorrect (never repeat a note name)

B♭ C C♯ D♯

Correct

B♭ C D♭ E♭

Incorrect (never skip a note name)

E F♯ A♭ B♭

Correct

E F♯ G♯ A♯

Exercise 17.1. Tetrachord Spelling

1. Leave the dotted circles blank. In the solid circles, write the letter names first (A B C D). Then add accidentals as needed to express the correct intervals.

A A
A A

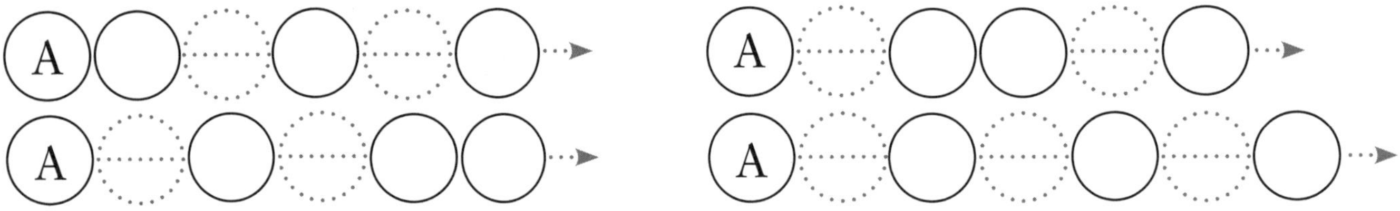

2. Fill in the tetrachord. Leave the dotted circles blank. In the solid circles, write the letter names first. Then add accidentals as needed to express the correct intervals.

D D
D D

G G
G G

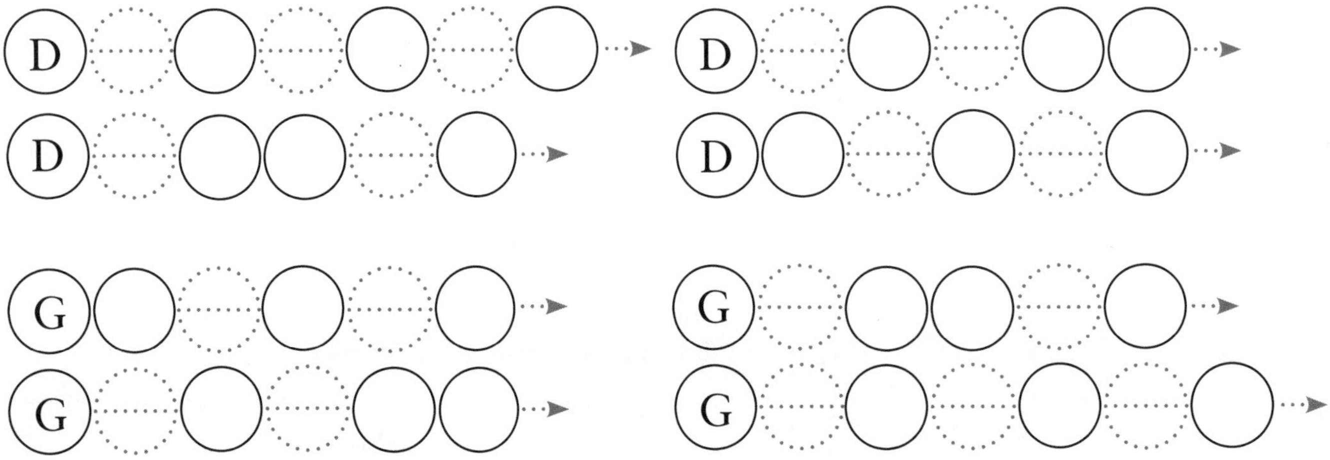

LESSON 17.2

The Four Tetrachords

There are four common modes of tetrachords—major, minor, Phrygian, and Lydian—and they each have a half step in a different place. The major tetrachord begins with two major seconds and ends with a minor second between the third and fourth notes. In a minor tetrachord, the minor second is between the second and third notes, as shown below.

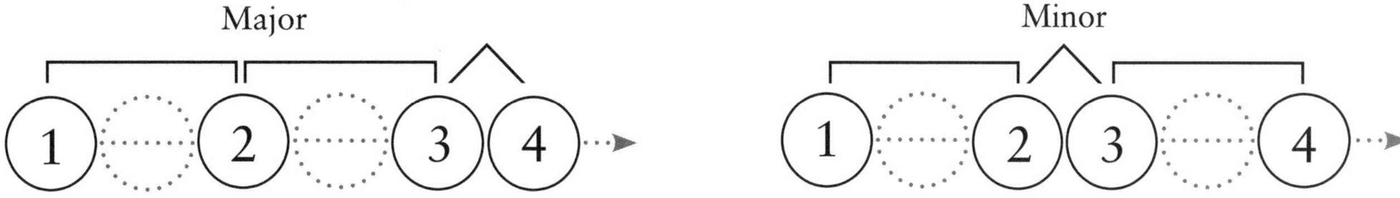

In the Phrygian tetrachord, the minor second is between 1 and 2. Lydian has no minor second at all.

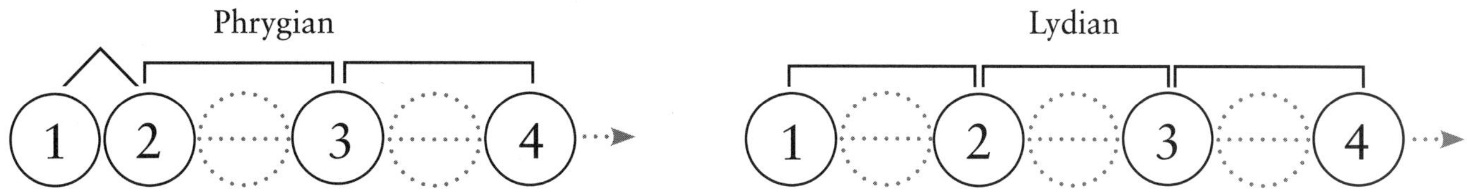

Tetrachords are identified by the name of the note in the first circle *and* the mode. For example, the first note in the tetrachord below is G and the half step is between the second and third notes, which makes it a minor tetrachord. So this tetrachord is identified as a G minor tetrachord.

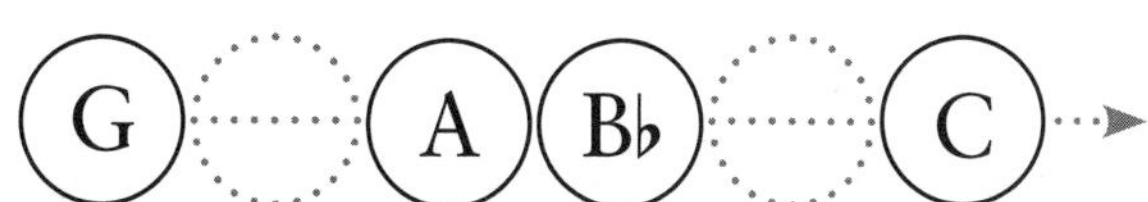

Exercise 17.2. The Four Tetrachords

1. Write the full name for each tetrachord, including the name of the first note and the mode of the tetrachord. The first one has been done for you.

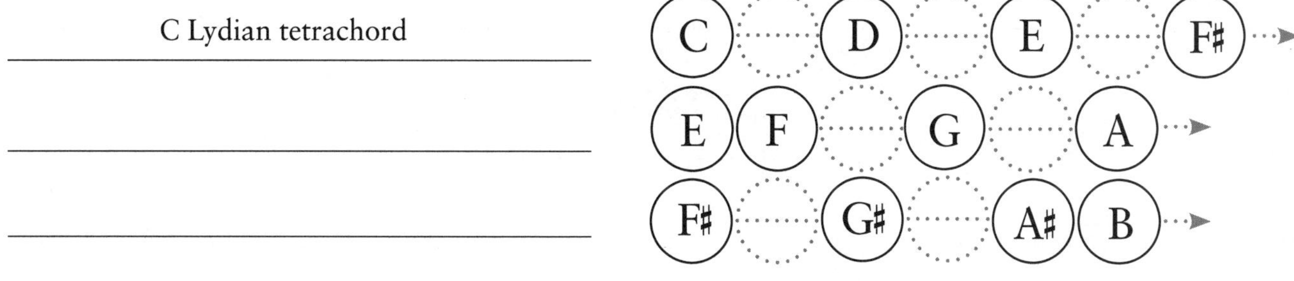

2. Finish writing the note names in the circles of the tetrachords below. Then in the spaces on the left, write the name and mode of each tetrachord.

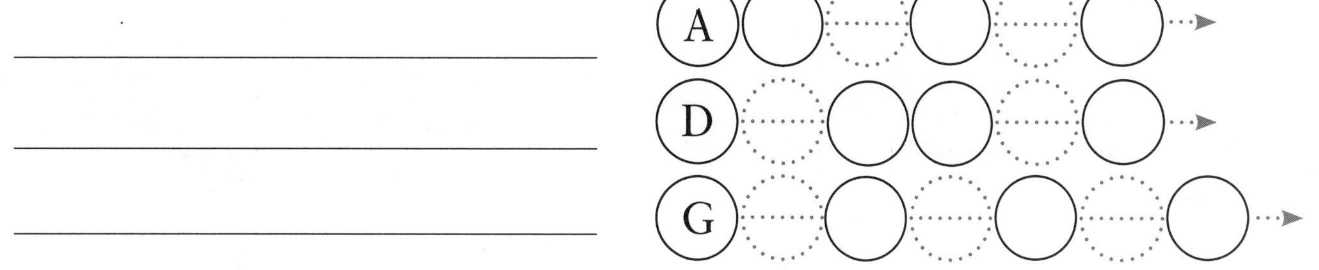

Exercise 17.2. The Four Tetrachords (cont.)

3. Write the name of the first note of the tetrachord in the circle. Then draw the remaining three circles, leaving a space between circles when there is a whole step. Finally, write in the names of the remaining notes of the tetrachord. The first one has been done for you.

Example: G Minor Tetrachord (G) ··· (A)(B♭) ··· (C) ···►

E♭ Major Tetrachord ( ) ···►

F♯ Phrygian Tetrachord ( ) ···►

E Lydian Tetrachord ( ) ···►

4. Finish writing the note names in the circles of the tetrachords below. Then in the spaces on the left, write the name and mode of each tetrachord.

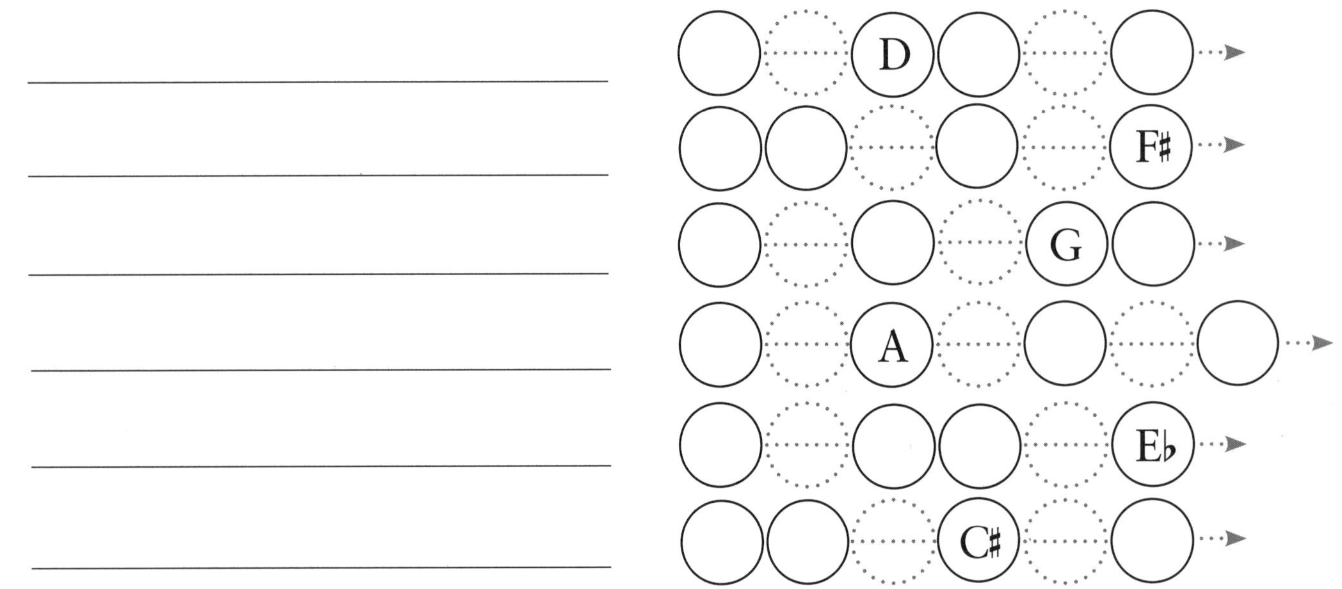

LESSON 17.3

Major and Minor Thirds

A **third** is made up of two notes that skip a note on the staff, such as A to C or D to F. On the staff below are many different types of thirds. Notice how thirds skip from one line to the next line, or from one space to the next space.

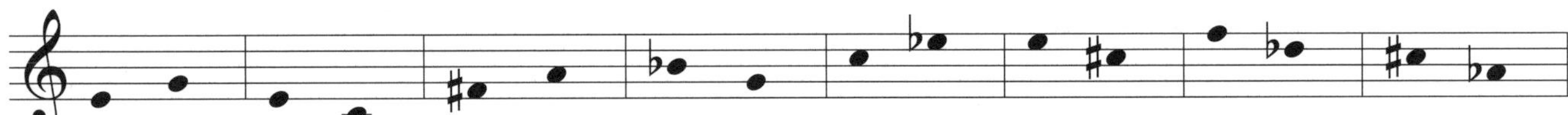

Major thirds are a half step bigger than minor thirds. A major third is two whole steps, and a minor third is one-and-a-half whole steps, as shown here.

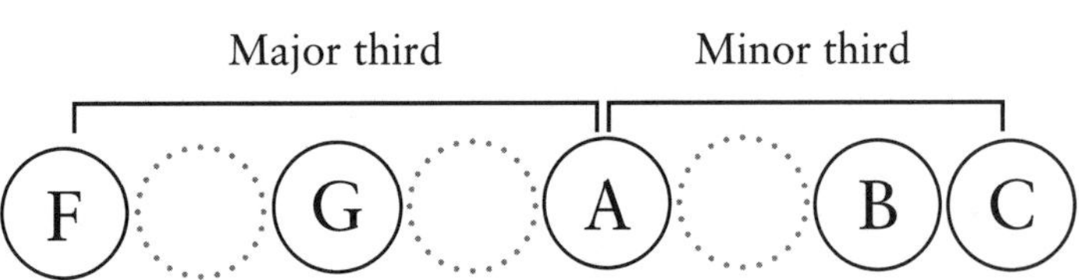

Exercise 17.3. Major and Minor Thirds

1. Each measure below has a third in it. Write a lowercase "m" over the measures with a minor third and a capital "M" over the measures with a major third. You may want to sketch out a fingerboard map to help you determine each interval, step by step.

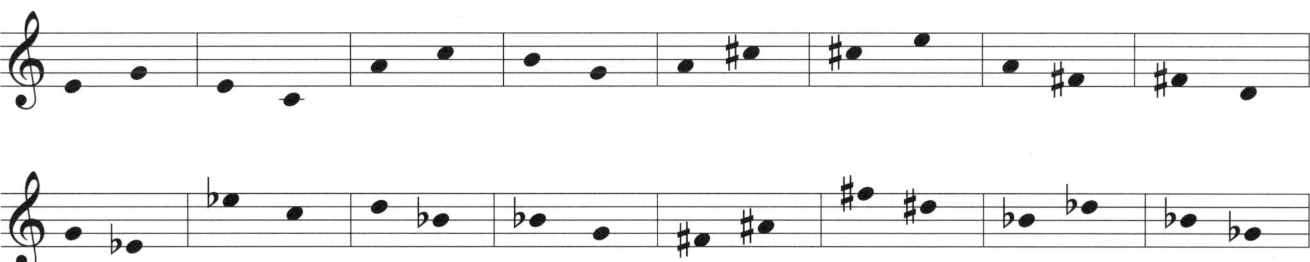

2. In each measure below, write the note that is a *minor third higher* than the given note. HINT: Draw the notehead first, and then determine if you need to add an accidental to make the third minor. Not all answers will require accidentals; some will be natural. The first measure of each line has been done for you.

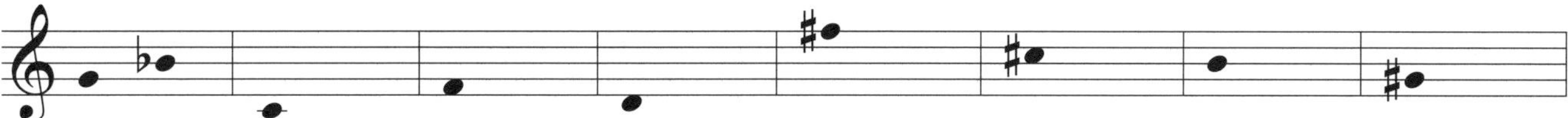

3. In each measure below, write the note that is a *major third higher* than the given note.

4. In each measure below, write the note that is a *minor third lower* than the given note.

5. In each measure below, write the note that is a *major third lower* than the given note.

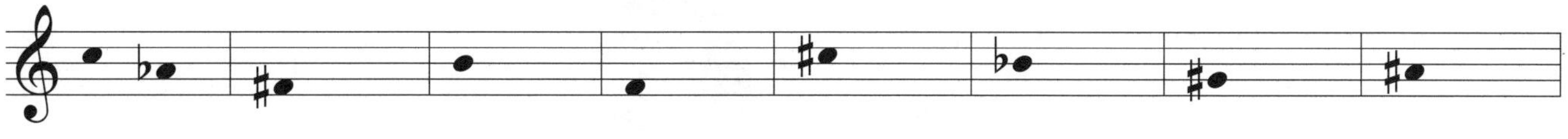

Unit 17 Study Guide

On a separate piece of paper, answer the following questions:

1. Explain the difference between a minor third and a major third in terms of whole steps.
2. What notes are a minor third above A, B, C, D, E, F, and G? What notes are a minor third below?
3. What notes are a major third above A, B, C, D, E, F, and G? What notes are a major third below?
4. Name the four tetrachords introduced in this unit, and explain how each is different from the others.
5. Draw seven major tetrachords, each one starting on a different letter: A, B, C, D, E, F, and G.
6. Draw seven minor, seven Phrygian, and seven Lydian tetrachords, each starting on a different letter: A, B, C, D, E, F, and G.

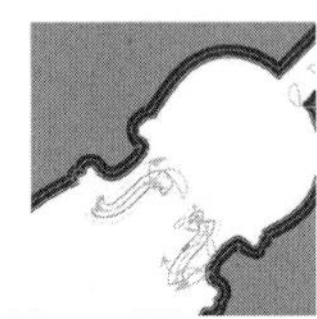

Unit 18. Compound Meter with Sixteenth Notes

LESSON 18.1

Compound Meter Review

In the first row of boxes below, $\frac{2}{4}$, $\frac{3}{4}$, and $\frac{4}{4}$ are examples of **simple meter**, which means that the beat is divided into two equal parts; if the quarter note gets the beat, the beat is divided into two eighth notes. In **compound meter** the beat is divided into three equal parts; the pulse is usually a dotted quarter note, which is divided equally into three eighth notes. $\frac{6}{8}$ typically has two beats per measure, $\frac{9}{8}$ has three beats per measure, and $\frac{12}{8}$ has four. Remember:

- In **duple meter**, the beats are *grouped* in twos. In **triple meter**, the beats are *grouped* in threes.
- In **simple meter**, the beat is *divided* into two. In **compound meter**, the beat is *divided* into three.

	Two Beats (*Duple Meter*)	Three Beats (*Triple Meter*)	Four Beats (*Duple Meter*)
Simple Meter (*beat divided into two*)	2/4 ♩ ♩ 2/4 ♫ ♫	3/4 ♩ ♩ ♩ 3/4 ♫ ♫ ♫	4/4 ♩ ♩ ♩ ♩ 4/4 ♫ ♫ ♫ ♫
Compound Meter (*beat divided into three*)	6/8 ♩. ♩. 6/8 ♪♪♪ ♪♪♪	9/8 ♩. ♩. ♩. 9/8 ♪♪♪ ♪♪♪ ♪♪♪	12/8 ♩. ♩. ♩. ♩. 12/8 ♪♪♪ ♪♪♪ ♪♪♪ ♪♪♪

In compound meters, the numbers refer to characteristics of the beat's division and not the beat itself.

In compound meters, the upper number always tells us *how many* divisions are in a measure.

The lower number tells us what *note value* gets the division. An 8 on the bottom means the eighth note is the division and the dotted quarter gets the beat.

$\frac{6}{8}$ = 2/♩. = 2 ♩. beats per measure

$\frac{9}{8}$ = 3/♩. = 3 ♩. beats per measure

$\frac{12}{8}$ = 4/♩. = 4 ♩. beats per measure

Exercise 18.1. Compound Meter Review

1. In each measure below, write the time signature that is illustrated by the rhythm in that measure. Some measures are expressed with eighth notes and some with dotted quarter notes.

Exercise 18.1. Compound Meter Review (cont.)

2. In each measure below, write the correct number of *eighth notes* to illustrate the time signature.

9/8 | 6/8 | 12/8 |

3. In each measure below, write the correct number of *dotted quarter notes* to illustrate the time signature.

12/8 | 9/8 | 6/8 |

4. 6/8 has _____ beats per measure. 9/8 has _____ beats per measure. 12/8 has _____ beats per measure.

5. Write stems over each beat in the last four measures. The stem goes directly over a note or rest. Notes longer than one beat should have the correct number of additional stems spaced evenly before the next note.

1 2 3 4 1 2 3 4

12/8

6. Follow the steps below to write eighth note stems, beams, and beat numbers in compound meter.
   - Step 1: Write eighth note stems over the notes, as shown in the first two measures. Notes longer than an eighth note should have the correct number of stems spaced evenly before the next note.
   - Step 2: Add beams to each group of three eighth note stems.
   - Step 3: Write the beat numbers over the first eighth note of each beamed group. The first two measures have been done for you.

7. The music below is in 9/8. There should be three beats (three groups of three eighth notes) per measure. Write the eighth note stems, then add beams, and write the beat numbers over the first note in each beam. Then perform the rhythm with your bow hand while counting in 9/8.

8. In the first measure below, how many eighth note stems are in the dotted half note? _____How many are in the dotted half rest? _____ How many beats are in the dotted half note and rest combined? _____ Write the stems first, and then add the beams and beat numbers. In 12/8 there should be four beats (four groups of three eighth notes) per measure. Then perform the rhythm with your bow hand while counting in 12/8.

LESSON 18.2

Sixteenth Note Rhythms in Compound Meter

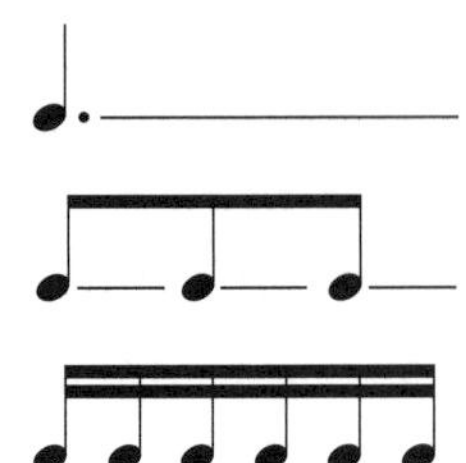

In compound meter, the beat is divided into three eighth notes and subdivided into six sixteenth notes. The beams group notes into beats, so sixteenth notes are beamed in groups of six, as shown to the right.

When counting eighth note rhythms in compound meter, use your teacher's counting method or the traditional counting system: 1 + a, 2 + a (*pronounced "1-an-da, 2-an-da"*). Counting sixteenth note rhythms in compound meter requires a little practice, but it can be done. Count "1-na-AN-na-DA-na, 2-na-AN-na-DA-na." Practice counting in eighths and sixteenths below.

Practice counting sixteenth note rhythms in compound meter. Then perform the rhythm example below with your bow hand while counting sixteenths to measure time.

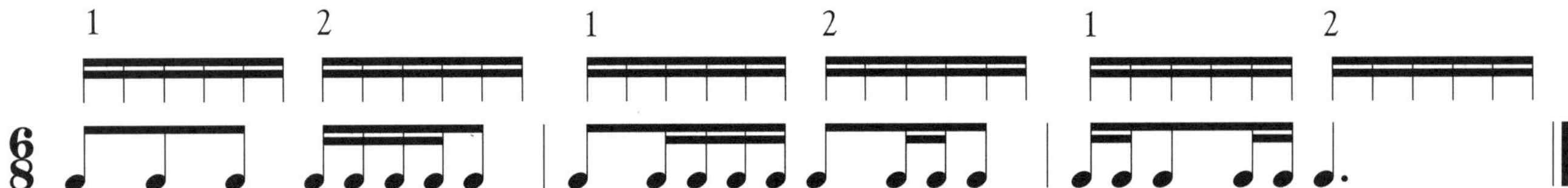

Exercise 18.2. Sixteenth Note Rhythms in Compound Meter

1. Follow the steps below to write sixteenth note stems, beams, and beat numbers in compound meter.
   - Step 1: Write sixteenth note stems over the notes in measures 2 and 3. Measure 1 has been done for you.
   - Step 2: Add double beams to each group of *six* sixteenth note stems.
   - Step 3: Write the beat numbers over the first note of each beamed group.
   - Step 4: Perform the rhythm with your bow hand while counting sixteenths to measure time.

2. In the first measure below, how many sixteenths go into a quarter note? _____ A dotted quarter note? _____ Finish writing sixteenth note stems, beams, and beat numbers. Then perform the rhythm while counting.

Exercise 18.2. Sixteenth Note Rhythms in Compound Meter (cont.)

3. In the first measure below, how many sixteenths go into a dotted eighth note? _____ Finish writing sixteenth note stems, beams, and beat numbers. Then perform the rhythm while counting.

4. In the first measure below, how many sixteenths go into a dotted eighth rest? _____ Finish writing sixteenth note stems, beams, and beat numbers. Then perform the rhythm while counting.

5. In the first measure below, how many sixteenths go into a syncopated eighth note? _____ Finish writing sixteenth note stems, beams, and beat numbers. Then perform the rhythm while counting.

6. Challenge: In $\frac{9}{8}$ there are three beats (three groups of six sixteenth notes) per measure. Write the sixteenth note stems, beams, and beat numbers (1 2 3). Then perform the rhythm while counting.

7. Challenge: In $\frac{12}{8}$ there are four beats (four groups of six sixteenth note stems) per measure. Write the sixteenth note stems, beams, and beat numbers (1 2 3 4). Then perform the rhythm while counting.

Unit 18 Study Guide

On a separate piece of paper, answer Questions 1–3. For additional practice, try Questions 4 and 5.

1. How is compound meter different from simple meter? How is duple meter different from triple meter? How is compound meter different from triple meter?
2. What do the top and bottom numbers in a compound meter time signature tell us? How is this different from the numbers of a simple meter time signature? Use time signatures to explain your answer.
3. In math, $\frac{3}{4}$ and $\frac{6}{8}$ are the same. Why are they not the same in music?
4. Count and perform the rhythms in this unit for a stand partner or friend.
5. Find sight-reading exercises or concert music with sixteenth note rhythms in compound meter. Then mark the music with sixteenth note stems, beams, and beat numbers, and perform the rhythms while counting.

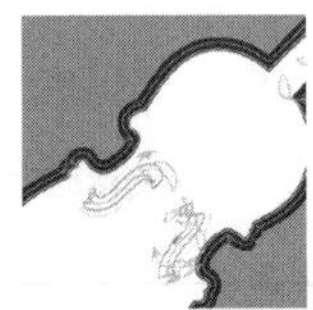

Unit 19. Mozart and the Modern Bow

LESSON 19.1

The History of the Bow

Around a thousand years ago, musicians began tying rosined horsehair to both ends of a stick so tightly that the stick "bowed" outward. As the bow evolved, the hair at one end of the stick was attached to a block of wood called a frog that was clipped or screwed onto the bow. These early Baroque era bows (see below) varied greatly in shape and size, and they worked well for the shorter notes common in Renaissance and Baroque music. However, they did not work as well for the longer notes required in music of the late Classical and early Romantic eras.

Between 1760 and 1780, a French bow maker named **François Tourte** (1747–1835) standardized the length, weight, size, and shape of the bows into the design we still use today (see below). He used Pernambuco wood from Brazil to make his bows longer, stronger, and better balanced at both ends. Instead of carving a concave bow, Tourte heated and bent the stick into a convex shape using a technique known as cambering. He also modernized the frog by adding a tightening screw to adjust the tension of the hair, and he added a small block of wood in the frog to spread the hair evenly into a flat ribbon.

The violin bow is the longest and lightest bow in the violin family. Viola and cello bows are shorter and heavier to give them the added strength to move their bigger strings. Many orchestral bass players use a German bow (see below) that is held underneath the stick, and they prefer its superior strength and power. Other bass players use Tourte's French bow design to perform faster, more virtuosic solos.

The new Tourte bow design enabled players to produce a variety of new bow strokes and articulations. Since Tourte and his contemporaries were French, many of the new terms—like **détaché** and **sautillé**—are also French. There are Italian bowing terms as well, like **spiccato, sul tasto,** and **sul ponticello.** In the glossary, you'll find definitions for these terms.

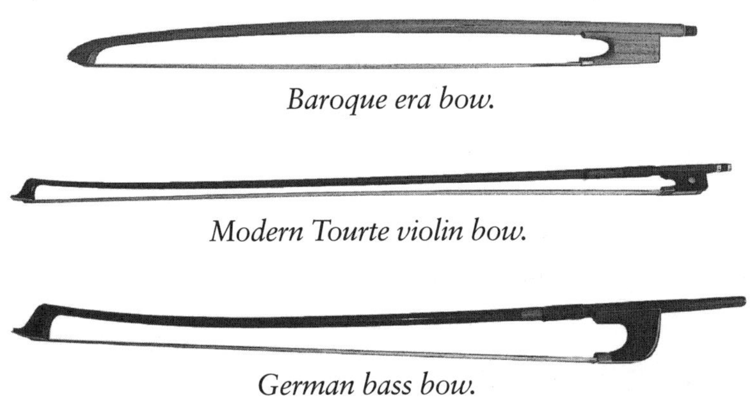

Baroque era bow.

Modern Tourte violin bow.

German bass bow.

Exercise 19.1. The History of the Bow

1. Who is credited with developing the design of the modern bow, and what made his bows better? __________

2. Why do some bass players prefer the German bow? __________

LESSON 19.2

Wolfgang Amadeus Mozart

Wolfgang Amadeus Mozart (1756–1791) was one of the most influential composers of the **Classical era** (1730–1820). In his short life, Mozart wrote more than six hundred works, including twenty-two operas, forty-one symphonies, many **concertos**, chamber pieces, and choral works. His unusual ability to write moving, sophisticated melodies naturally contributed to his advancements in both opera and the concerto. His twenty-three piano concertos helped popularize the genre, and his wind concertos—particularly for oboe, clarinet, bassoon, and French horn—remain among the most important concertos for those instruments today.

Mozart was born and raised in Salzburg, Austria. His father, Leopold Mozart, was a skilled violinist and teacher who wrote a well-respected textbook on the fundamental principles of violin playing. Leopold taught his son to play piano and violin at a very young age, and he immediately recognized his son's ingenious ability to remember melody, harmony, and style. Leopold toured Europe with his son to show off the boy's talent to princes, kings, and queens in exchange for money and gifts. During his travels Mozart met and learned from other accomplished composers, and he heard great music from a variety of countries. Mozart's exposure to the best music in Europe was an integral part of his education. He began composing at the age of six, and he wrote his first **symphony** at the age of eight and his first opera at twelve. He traveled with his father for eleven years, and during that time he wrote eight operas, twenty-one symphonies, and many other works.

By the age of seventeen Mozart was too old to earn money as a child prodigy, so he got a job as a court musician in his father's orchestra in Salzburg and continued writing symphonies, sonatas, chamber music, and choral works. He wrote all five of his violin concertos in the span of just nine months when he was nineteen. As his works gained popularity, Mozart started to travel again, this time on his own, looking for better work in Mannheim, Munich, and Paris. Mozart spent so much time away from his Salzburg job that he was eventually fired. This embarrassed Mozart's father, and after they had a serious falling out Mozart left Salzburg and moved to Vienna, Austria.

Mozart married Constanze Weber when he was twenty-six, and they had six children, but only two survived infancy. In 1784 Mozart became friends with **Haydn**, and Mozart dedicated six of his **string quartets** to the elder composer. Mozart composed and performed many piano concertos, and his concerts made him famous in Vienna. In the last five years of his life, Mozart was extremely productive, writing his most famous symphonies—Nos. 39, 40, and 41—and several operas, including *The Marriage of Figaro*, *Don Giovanni*, and *The Magic Flute*. He made good money but not enough to support his lavish lifestyle. In 1786 Mozart's financial struggles worsened and his health declined. In his final year, Mozart wrote *The Magic Flute*, his last piano concerto, a clarinet concerto, and a very popular motet, *Ave verum corpus*. He also began writing his *Requiem*, which he did not finish before dying at the age of thirty-five.

Unit 19 Study Guide

On a separate piece of paper, answer the following questions:

1. Who was François Tourte, and what made his bows better than Baroque era bows?
2. Why do some bass players prefer the German bow? How is it different from a French bow?
3. Describe the main contributions that Mozart made to the string music world.

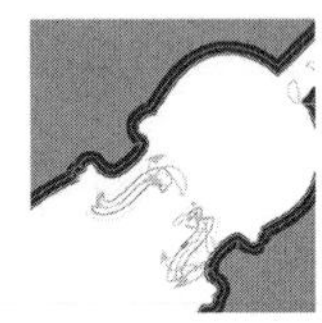

Unit 20. Major Scales in Sharp Keys

LESSON 20.1

How Major Scales Are Built

A major tetrachord has a stepwise pattern made of two major seconds and a minor second. A **major scale** is made of two major tetrachords separated by a whole step, as shown below. This pattern is the same for all major scales.

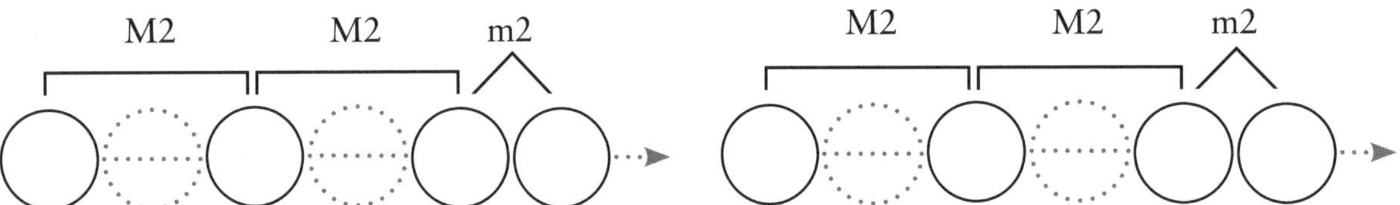

The C major scale below is built with a C tetrachord and a G tetrachord separated by a major second.

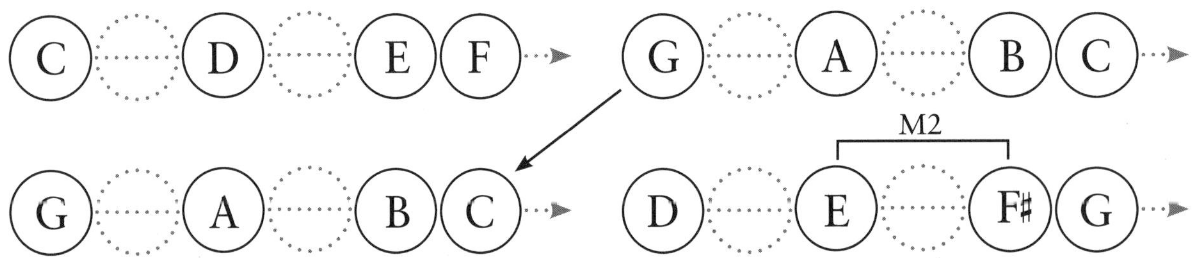

The G major scale is built with a G tetrachord and a D tetrachord separated by a major second. Notice how the seventh note of the G scale is an F♯, because it must be a major second higher than E.

Exercise 20.1. How Major Scales Are Built

1. The second tetrachord of the G scale (above) is the D tetrachord that begins the D major scale. Complete the D scale below and continue building the remaining scales on this page. You will notice that the seventh note of each scale is a new sharp that stays in the remaining scales.

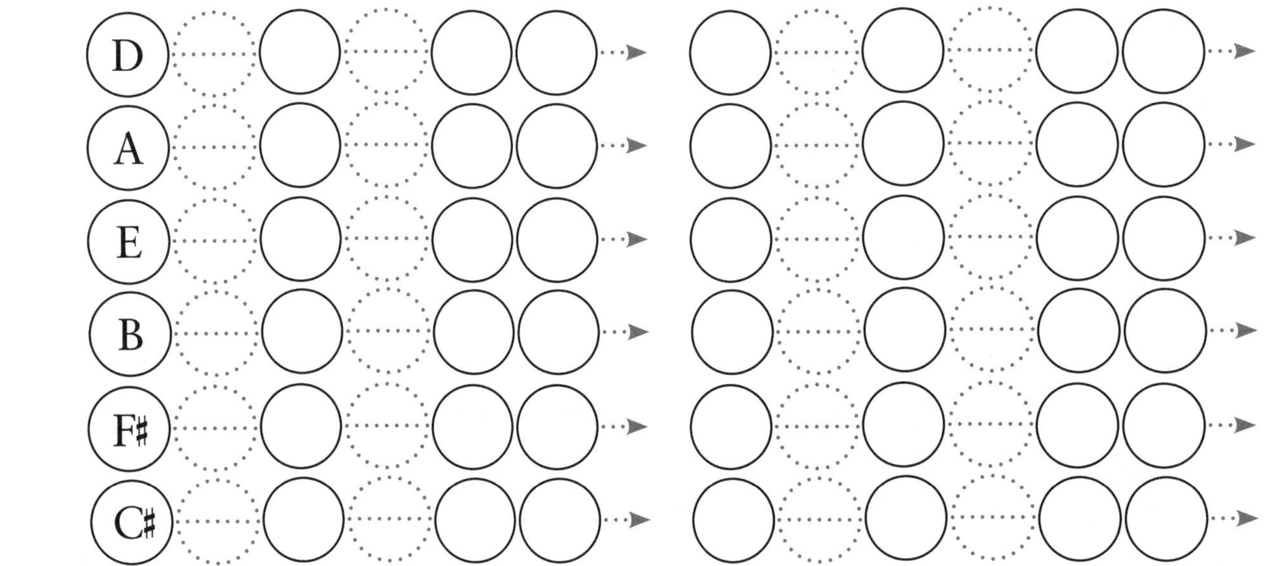

Exercise 20.1. How Major Scales Are Built (cont.)

2. On the staves below, write out the scales that you built on the previous page. Write sharps (♯) in front of the notes that are sharp. The first two have been done for you.

LESSON 20.2

Scale Degrees

Scale degrees identify specific notes in a scale based on their order in the scale. The first scale degree is the first note of the scale; the third scale degree is the third note, and so on. Melodies sound finished or "resolved" when they end on the first scale degree, which is why it is often called the "resting tone." Scales are named by their first scale degree. For example, an F♯ scale begins and ends with F♯. Since the first and eighth note of a scale are the same, we replace the eighth scale degree with a 1 again to avoid confusion.

Exercise 20.2. Scale Degrees

1. Which major scale degrees are separated by only a half step? _____ - _____ and _____ - _____
2. What is another name for the first scale degree?______________________________
3. What is the second scale degree of a: D scale? ________ A scale?________ F♯ scale?________
4. What is the seventh scale degree of a: G scale? ________ D scale?________ A scale?________
5. In the table below, write the name of the key (first scale degree) and the seventh scale degree associated with the key that has the number of sharps indicated below.

Number of sharps in key	0	1	2	3	4	5	6	7
First scale degree (name of key)								
Seventh scale degree								

LESSON 20.3

The Order of Sharps

Check the answers for Question 6 of Exercise 20.2. The order of the seventh scale degrees of the major sharp keys are as follows: F♯, C♯, G♯, D♯, A♯, E♯, B♯. This is known as the order of sharps, and it can be easily remembered with a mnemonic device: **F**ather **C**harles **G**oes **D**own **A**nd **E**nds **B**attle. In Book 1 you learned that the **key signature** is a group of sharps or flats written after the clef that indicates which notes on the staff should be performed sharp or flat. When writing a key signature, sharps must be written in the order of sharps: F, C, G, D, A, E, and B.

C Major (0 ♯) G Major (1 ♯: F♯) D Major (2 ♯: F♯, C♯) A Major (3 ♯: F♯, C♯, G♯)

Sharp Key Signature Rule: The last sharp in each key signature is the seventh scale degree. To find the major key of a sharp key signature, just go up a minor second from the last sharp.

Exercise 20.3. The Order of Sharps

1. Next to the first clef below is the signature for the key of C♯ major. This key has seven sharps; every note is sharp. Write this key signature nine more times, each with the sharps on the correct lines and spaces and with the correct order of sharps. Use the first example as a model, and repeat the mnemonic device from above each time you rewrite the key signature.

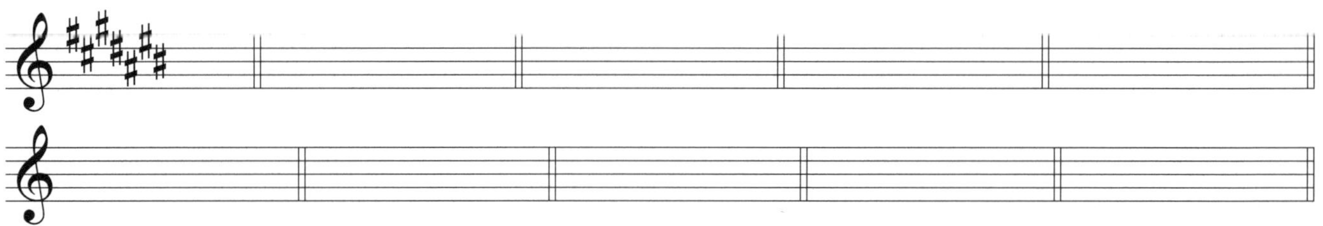

2. Use the mnemonic device to help you write the key signatures of the keys indicated under each measure. Then write a whole note on the first scale degree of the key, which is a minor second higher than the last sharp (the seventh scale degree.) The key of G has been done for you.

Unit 20 Study Guide

On a separate piece of paper, complete the following tasks:

1. Draw a major scale diagram with scale degrees, similar to the diagram in Lesson 20.2.
2. Write the order of sharps. Write the names of the major sharp keys in order from no sharps to seven.
3. Explain what scale degrees are. Explain why the first scale degree is called the "resting tone."
4. Explain how to find the name of the key (first scale degree) when looking at a sharp key signature.

On a separate sheet of staff paper, complete the following tasks:

5. Write a one-octave scale in each of the sharp keys using accidentals (not key signatures).
6. Write the key signature for each of the seven sharp keys using the correct order of sharps.

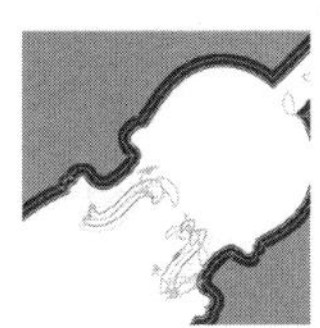

Unit 21. Major Scales in Flat Keys

LESSON 21.1

How Flat Major Scales Are Built

The C major tetrachord is the first tetrachord in a C major scale, but it is also the second tetrachord of a different major scale. By filling in the notes of the first tetrachord of the new scale, we learn that the C major tetrachord is the second half of an F major scale, as shown below.

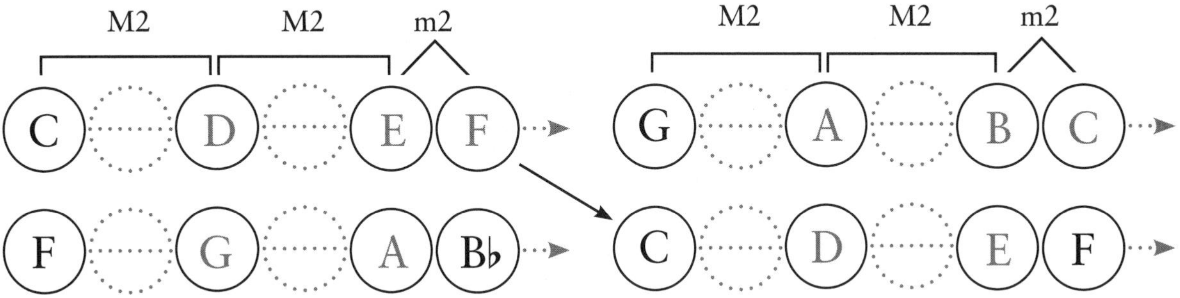

Exercise 21.1. How Flat Major Scales Are Built

1. The F major tetrachord (in the F scale shown above) is also the second tetrachord of a B♭ major scale (shown below). Finish writing in the note names of the B♭ scale below and the remaining scales on this page. Notice how the fourth note of each scale is the new flat that stays in the remaining scales.

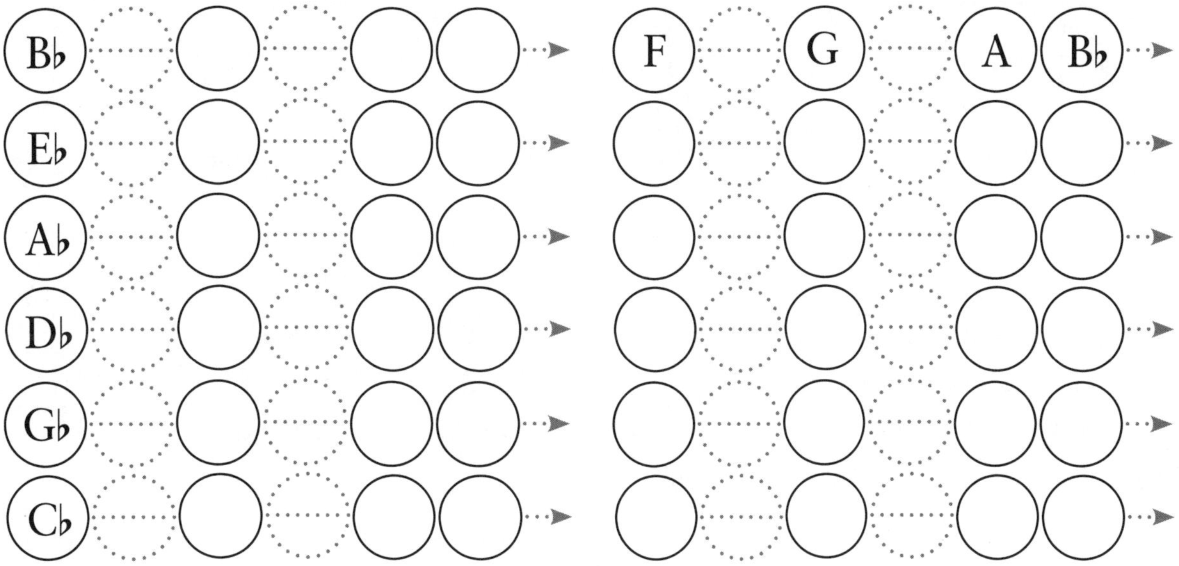

B♭ ___ ___ ___ → F G A B♭ →
E♭ ___ ___ ___ → ___ ___ ___ ___ →
A♭ ___ ___ ___ → ___ ___ ___ ___ →
D♭ ___ ___ ___ → ___ ___ ___ ___ →
G♭ ___ ___ ___ → ___ ___ ___ ___ →
C♭ ___ ___ ___ → ___ ___ ___ ___ →

2. In the table below, write the names of the first and fourth scale degrees in the keys with the number of flats indicated below. The first two have been done for you.

Number of flats in key	0	1	2	3	4	5	6	7
First scale degree (name of key)	C	F						
Fourth scale degree	F	B♭						

Exercise 21.1. How Flat Major Scales Are Built (cont.)

3. On the staves below, write out the scales that you built on the previous page. Write flats (♭) in front of the notes that are flat. The first two have been done for you.

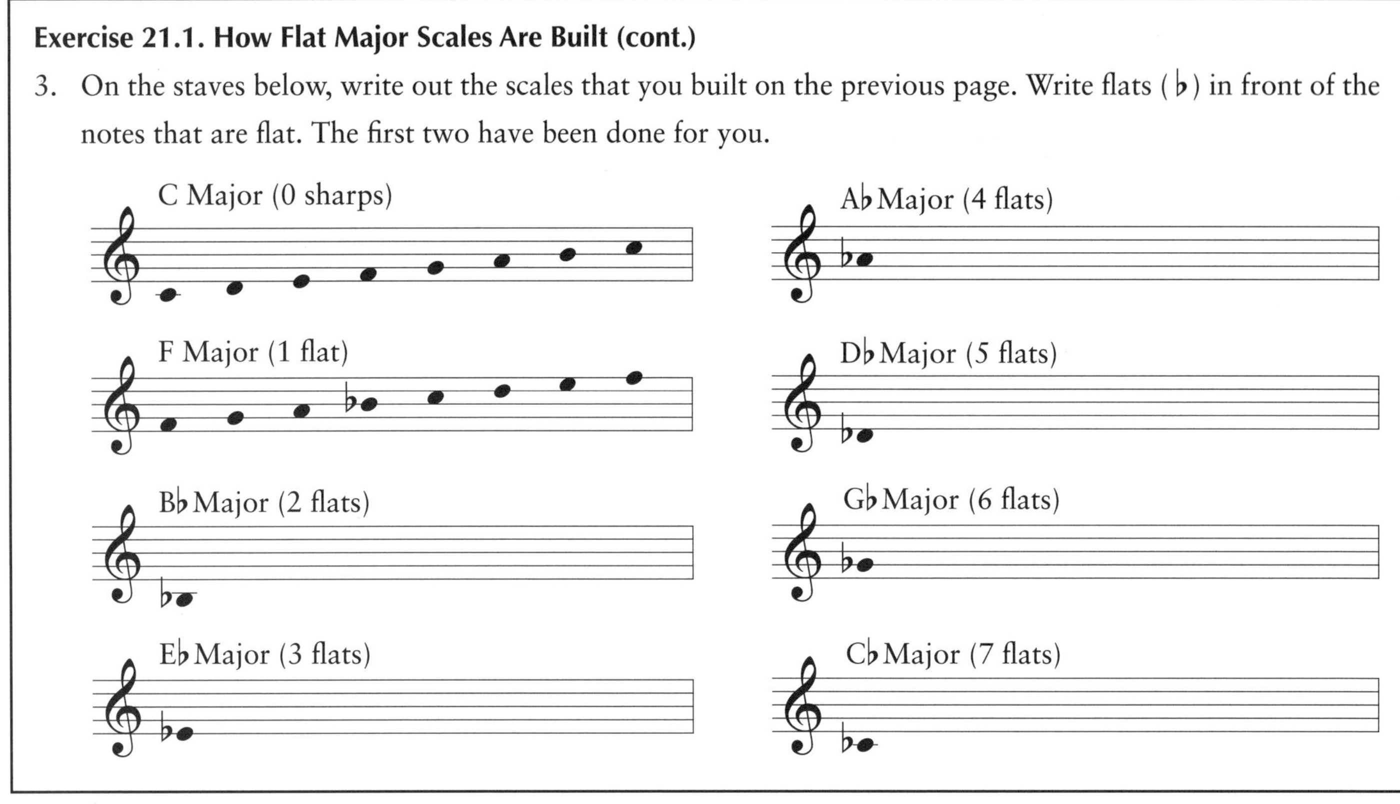

LESSON 21.2

The Order of Flats

In the table from Question 2 of Exercise 21.2, the order of the fourth scale degrees are as follows: B♭, E♭, A♭, D♭, G♭, C♭, F♭. This is known as the order of flats, and in flat key signatures the flats are always written in that order. It can be easily remembered with a mnemonic device: **B**attle **E**nds **A**nd **D**own **G**oes **C**harles' **F**ather.

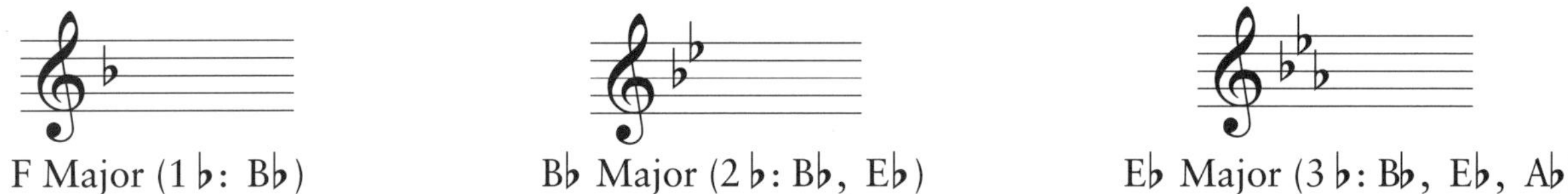

F Major (1 ♭: B♭)   B♭ Major (2 ♭: B♭, E♭)   E♭ Major (3 ♭: B♭, E♭, A♭)

There are three rules that are very helpful for remembering key signatures:

1. Flat Key Signature Rule: The name of the key is the same as the second-to-last flat in the key signature. In the key signature to the right, the second-to-last flat is A♭, so this is the key signature for A♭ major. Be sure to include the ♭ in the name of the key because A and A♭ are different keys. There are two exceptions to this rule:

- The key of F major only has one flat. This is easy to remember because the word *flat* begins with the letter F.
- The key signature for C major has no flats or sharps.

2. The Rule of Sevens: Keys that share the same letter name have sharps and flats that always add up to seven. For example, the key of G has one sharp, so the key of G♭ has six flats, because 1 + 6 = 7. The key of D has two sharps, so the key of D♭ must have five flats, because 2 + 5 = 7. The key with seven sharps is C♯ major. The key with seven flats is C♭ major. Do you remember the key in which all seven notes are natural?

3. The Inversion Principle: In the keys that share the same letter name, the notes that are natural in one key are the notes that have sharps or flats in the other key. For example, the key of A has three sharps, which means the key of A♭ has four flats, and those four flat notes are the four notes that were not sharp in the key of A. See below:

A	B	C♯	D	E	F♯	G♯	A
A♭	B♭	C	D♭	E♭	F	G	A♭

Exercise 21.2. The Order of Flats

1. Write the key signature for C♭ major ten times. Write all seven flats on the correct lines and spaces and in the correct order—neatness counts. The first one has been done for you. Repeat the mnemonic device (**B**attle **E**nds . . .) for each key signature.

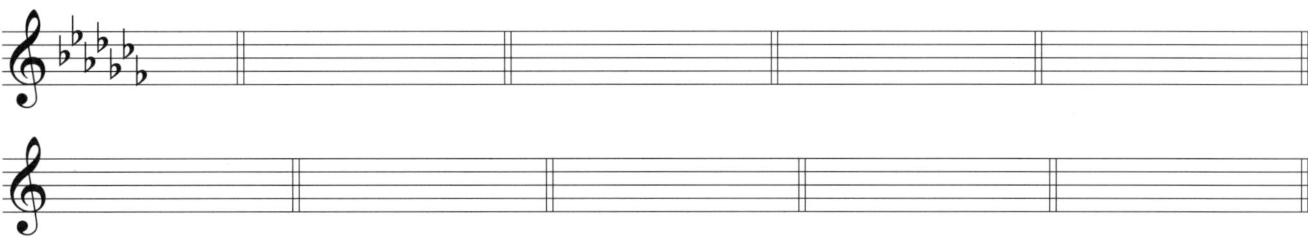

2. Use the mnemonic device to help you write the key signatures of the keys indicated under each measure. Then write a whole note on the same line or space as the second-to-last flat; this is the resting tone and name of the major key. The keys of F and B♭ have been done for you.

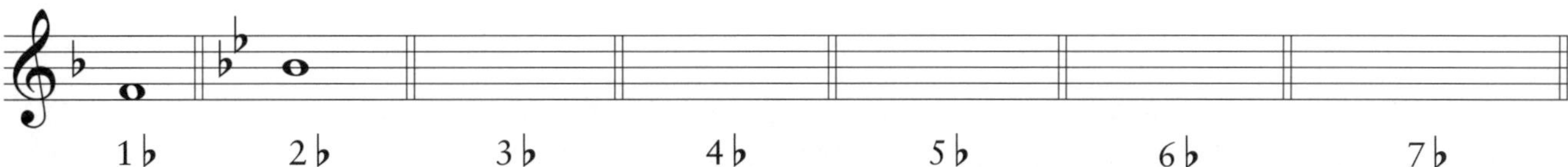

1♭ 2♭ 3♭ 4♭ 5♭ 6♭ 7♭

3. Look at the exercise above and use the Rule of Sevens to answer the following: If the key of F has one flat, the key of F♯ must have _____ sharps. Using the same rule, the key of B must have _____ sharps. E major has _____ sharps. A major has _____ sharps. D major has _____ sharps. G major has _____ sharps.
4. Use the Inversion Principle to answer the following: If the key of B♭ has two flats (B♭ and E♭), then the key of B must have the following sharp notes: ___________________________. Using the same rule, the key of E must have the following sharp notes: ___________________________.

Unit 21 Study Guide

On a separate sheet of paper, complete the following tasks:

1. Write out the order of flats and sharps.
2. Write the names of the major keys in order from seven flats to seven sharps.
3. Explain the rules for determining the name of the major key when looking at flat and sharp key signatures. What are the exceptions to the two rules?
4. Explain the Rule of Sevens and the Inversion Principle.

On a separate sheet of staff paper, complete the following tasks:

5. Write a one-octave scale in each of the flat and sharp keys using accidentals (not key signatures).
6. Write the key signatures of every flat and sharp key from seven flats to seven sharps.

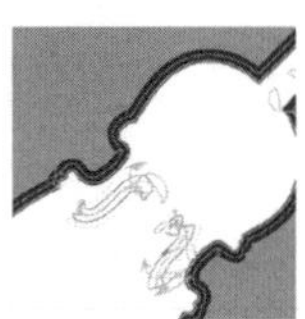

Unit 22. Creativity Projects

Exercise 22.1. The Cover Project

1. Find a group of three to five fun, collaborative friends and select a song by a non-classical artist that you like a lot. If you need help selecting a good song, ask your teacher. Listen to your song until you know it well. Then learn to play one verse and the chorus by ear on your instrument.
2. Next, create a "cover" of this song with your group. Determine who will play or sing the melody, bass line, and the other harmonies and rhythms.
3. Create a structure that works for your group. How many verses and choruses will your group play? How do you want the song to start and end? Will it have a bridge?
4. Rehearse and practice performing your cover project with your friends. When you are ready, create a video or perform the cover for your teacher or class.

Exercise 22.2. Creating An Arrangement

1. On a piece of staff paper, write down a folk song or holiday tune that you like. If you prefer, write your own melody. Then compose a short arrangement for a small group of two to four players. Keep it simple, and use your instrument to help you. Write out the melody and show it to your teacher for approval and feedback before adding other instruments. Make sure that your key signature and time signature agree with your melody.
2. To accompany your melody, you will need harmony and a bass line that is different from the melody but still sounds good when played together. Write down a few ideas, and then ask a friend to play your harmony or bass line while you play the melody. Each instrument gets its own staff; do not put two instruments on the same staff. Keep the music in a comfortable range and easily playable on the instruments in your ensemble. As you get more accomplished at writing, you can give the melody to different instruments while others share the responsibility of playing the harmony and bass line.

3. Each staff should have a clef and a key signature. The first staff should also have a time signature after the key signature. Use bar lines to divide the music into measures with the correct number of beats, and write a double bar at the end of your work. Regularly show your work to your teacher, especially if and when you have any questions about how to proceed.
4. When you are finished, create a video or perform the composition for your teacher or the class.

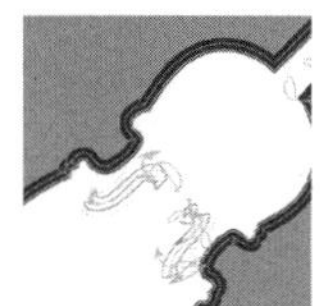

Unit 23. Half Note Time Signatures

LESSON 23.1

Half Note Time Signatures

So far we have studied time signatures like $\frac{2}{4}$, $\frac{3}{4}$, and $\frac{4}{4}$ with a quarter note beat, as well as compound time signatures like $\frac{6}{8}$, $\frac{9}{8}$, and $\frac{12}{8}$ with a dotted quarter note beat. In this lesson we introduce time signatures with a half note beat. Since a half note is divided into two quarter notes, most of these meters are simple meters, and the numbers in their time signatures refer to the number of beats in the measure.

The upper number tells us how many beats are in a measure, and the lower number tells us what note value gets the beat. The 2 on the bottom means the half note gets the beat.

𝄵 is called "cut time" and is the same as $\frac{2}{2}$.

$\frac{2}{2}$

𝄵 = $\frac{2}{2}$ = $\frac{2}{𝅗𝅥}$ = 2 𝅗𝅥 beats per measure

$\frac{3}{2}$ = $\frac{3}{𝅗𝅥}$ = 3 𝅗𝅥 beats per measure

$\frac{4}{2}$ = $\frac{4}{𝅗𝅥}$ = 4 𝅗𝅥 beats per measure

Below you can see that a dotted whole note (𝅝.) is the same length as three half notes. A breve, or double whole note (𝅜), is as long as four half notes (or two whole notes).

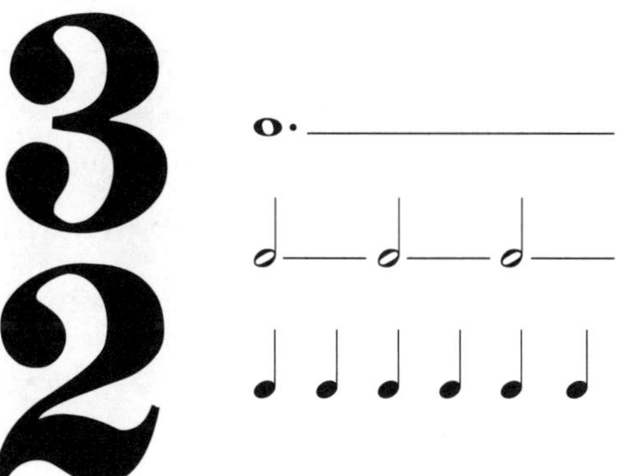

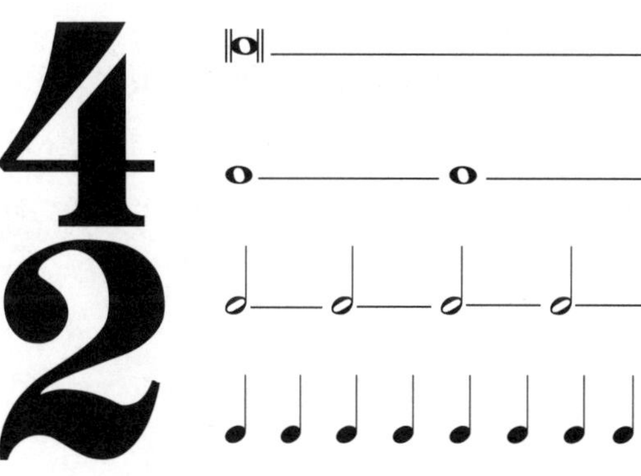

In these meters a whole rest can mean one of two things: If the whole rest is in a measure with no other symbols, then it lasts the full measure. If there are other symbols in a measure with a whole rest, the whole rest lasts only as long as four quarter notes. You will sometimes see a dotted whole rest, which lasts as long as three half notes.

Exercise 23.1. Half Note Time Signatures

1. In the exercise below, how many beats are in a whole note? _____ A dotted whole note? _____ Finish the exercise by marking the half note beats with stems and beat numbers. Then perform the rhythm with your bow hand while counting the beat numbers.

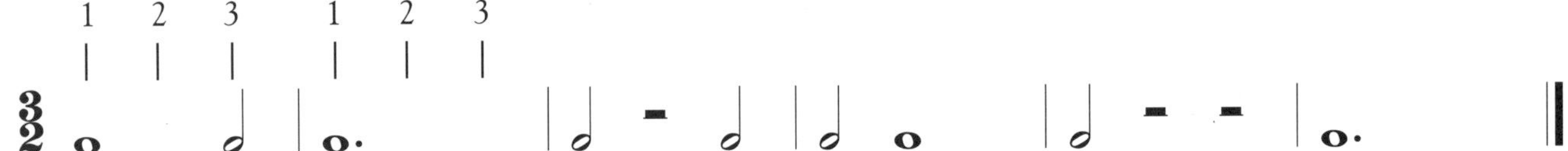

2. In the music example for Question 3 below, the note in the second measure is called a __________. It is as long as how many half notes?_____ Explain the difference in the length of the whole rests in measures 1 and 3. ______________________________

____

3. Finish writing the beat stems and numbers in the remaining measures. Then perform the rhythm with your bow hand while counting out the beats.

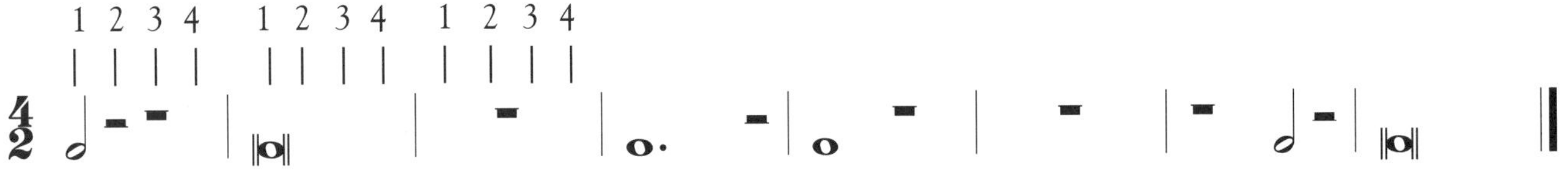

LESSON 23.2

Subdividing a Half Note Beat

In half note time signatures, quarter notes divide the beat in the same way that eighth notes divide quarter note beats. We can write beamed stems over the music to help us visualize how quarter notes are grouped into beats. We use a single beam to *divide* half note beats into two parts. Said another way: Write eighth note stems over the quarter note values, as shown below.

Exercise 23.2. Subdividing a Half Note Beat

1. Cut time is performed quickly and is almost always counted (and felt) in two. Finish writing stems over the quarter note values and then beam the pairs of stems to show two beats/beams per measure. Write the beat numbers over each beam, and perform the rhythm with your bow hand while counting "1 + 2 +."

2. $\frac{3}{2}$ is generally performed and felt in a broad three. Finish writing stems over the quarter note values and then beam the pairs of stems to show three beats/beams per measure. Write the beat numbers over each beam, and perform the rhythm with your bow hand while counting "1 + 2 + 3 +."

Exercise 23.2. Subdividing a Half Note Beat (cont.)

Eighth notes subdivide a half note beat into four parts just as sixteenth notes subdivide quarter note beats. When eighth notes are present in half note time signatures, we use a double beam to *subdivide* the beats into four parts. Said another way: Write sixteenth note stems over the eighth notes as shown below.

3. How many subdivisions go into a dotted quarter below? _____ Cut time is often used in marches and is felt in two. It should have two beats (two groups of four sixteenth note stems) in each measure. Over the remaining measures, write sixteenth note stems, double beam the stems in groups of four, and write the beat numbers over each beam. Then perform the rhythm with your bow hand while counting "1 e + a, 2 e + a."

4. The example below is in 3/2, so it should have three beats (three groups of four sixteenth note stems) in each measure. Over the remaining measures, write sixteenth note stems, beams, and beat numbers. Then perform the rhythm while counting "1 e + a, 2 e + a, 3 e + a."

5. The example below is in 4/2, so it should have four beats (four groups of four sixteenth note stems) in each measure. Over the remaining measures, write sixteenth note stems, beams, and beat numbers. Then perform the rhythm while counting "1 e + a, 2 e + a, 3 e + a, 4 e + a."

LESSON 23.3

6/4 vs. 3/2

We have studied all of the common regular time signatures found in orchestral music except for one: 6/4. This time signature is a compound time signature, and its dotted half note beats are divided into three parts. Even though it has six quarter notes in a measure, it is a lot more like 6/8 than 3/2. See below.

	Quarter Note Division	Eighth Note Division
Two Beats (Compound Meter)	6/4 6/4	6/8 6/8
Three Beats (Simple Meter)	3/2 3/2	3/4 3/4

Exercise 23.3. $\frac{6}{4}$ vs. $\frac{3}{2}$

1. At the beginning of each measure below, write the time signature illustrated by the rhythm in that measure.

2. In each measure below, write the correct number of half notes or dotted half notes for each time signature.

3. $\frac{6}{4}$ is usually performed and felt in two groups of three. So it should have two beats (two groups of three eighth note stems) in each measure. Over the remaining measures, write eighth note stems, beams, and beat numbers like in measure 1. Then perform the rhythm while counting "1 + a, 2 + a."

4. As before, write the stems over the quarter note values and beam them in groups of three. Write the beat numbers, and perform the rhythm with your bow hand while counting "1 + a, 2 + a."

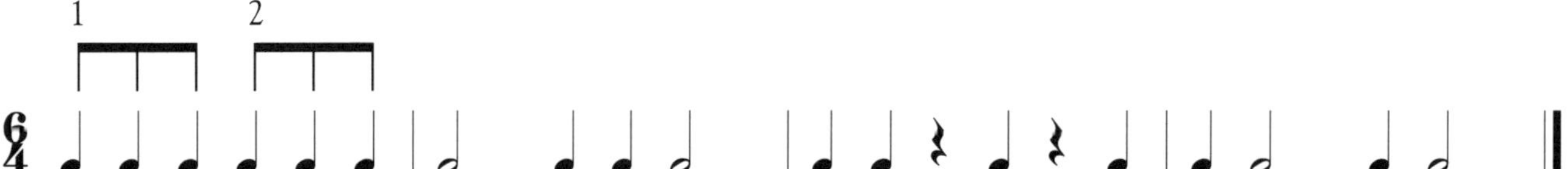

5. The rhythm below is in $\frac{3}{2}$, so it should have three beats (three groups of two eighth note stems) in each measure. Over the remaining measures, write eighth note stems, beams, and beat numbers. Then perform the rhythm while counting "1 +, 2 +, 3 +."

6. Now go back and perform the rhythm in Question 4 again while counting in $\frac{6}{4}$. You should notice that though they may look similar, $\frac{6}{4}$ feels very different than $\frac{3}{2}$. This is why it is important to know the difference between the two.

In a real performance situation, we don't put marks over every measure of our concert music. We use markings over the rhythms that give us trouble to help us visualize how the notes and beats are organized and meant to be performed.

LESSON 23.4

Triplets

In a **triplet**, three evenly spaced notes are put in a place where two notes usually go. Three triplet eighth notes fit into the space of two regular eighth notes. Three triplet quarter notes fit into the space of two normal quarter notes. In measures 2 and 3 below, you will see triplets marked with a "3" above the beam.

To write a triplet, we put a "3" over the group of eighth notes to signify that all three eighth notes should fit in the space of two eighths (or one quarter).

Exercise 23.4. Triplets

1. Write eighth note stems, beams, and beat numbers over the exercise below. There should be two eighth note stems per beat and four beats per measure. Then perform the rhythm with the bow hand while counting eighth notes.

2. Write quarter note stems and beat numbers over the exercise below. There should be four beats per measure. Then perform the rhythm with the bow hand while counting quarter notes.

Unit 23 Study Guide

On a separate piece of paper, answer Questions 1–3. For additional practice, try Questions 4 and 5.

1. How is $\frac{3}{4}$ similar to $\frac{3}{2}$? How is it different? Explain the similarities and differences between $\frac{2}{4}$ and $\frac{2}{2}$, as well as the differences and similarities between $\frac{6}{8}$ and $\frac{6}{4}$.
2. What do the numbers in half note time signatures tell us? How is this different from the numbers in a quarter note time signature? Use time signatures to explain your answer.
3. In math, $\frac{3}{2}$ and $\frac{6}{4}$ are the same. Why are they not the same in music?
4. Count and perform the rhythms in this unit for a stand partner or friend.
5. Find sight-reading exercises or concert music with half note meters. Then mark the music with stems, beams, and beat numbers, and perform the rhythms while counting.

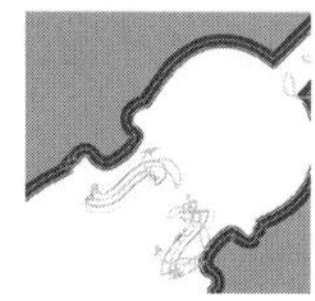

Unit 24. Musical Nationalism and Tchaikovsky

LESSON 24.1

Musical Nationalism

Early in the **Romantic era** (1800–1910) a new sentiment of national loyalty and identity spread across Europe. This sentiment came to be known as **nationalism**, and the arts were a powerful voice for this new movement. Some nationalist composers incorporated national folk songs and patriotic anthems into their orchestral music. Others used subtle compositional devices to create an ethnic character in their music. Composers continued to use nationalistic musical elements to inspire patriotism and national pride throughout the twentieth century and even still do so today. Some of the most notable nationalist composers and works are listed below.

Bedřich Smetana (1824–1884) was a Czech composer who wrote a collection of tone poems called *Ma Vlast* ("My Homeland"). These works depict Czech landscapes and folklore, and the second poem about a river, "The Moldau," is frequently performed by itself. Smetana paved the way for his successor, Antonín Dvořák (1841–1904), a Czech composer whose nationalist orchestral works include his *Czech Suite* and sixteen *Slavonic Dances*.

Edvard Grieg (1843–1907) incorporated Norwegian folk songs into his music. Several of his more popular works include the *Peer Gynt* suite, a piano concerto, and the *Holberg Suite*, which was written to celebrate the two hundredth anniversary of the birth of the Norwegian playwright Ludvig Holberg.

Jean Sibelius (1865–1957) was a Finnish composer best known for his Symphony No. 2, violin concerto, and a tone poem called *Finlandia*, which he wrote to protest Russian censorship in Finland's press. The beautiful melody in the middle of *Finlandia* is still frequently sung in Finland today.

Aaron Copland (1900–1990) was one of America's greatest classical composers. He used slow-moving harmonies and open textures to create images of the vast American landscape. He is best known for the work *Fanfare for the Common Man* and the music from two **ballets**. The first, *Appalachian Spring*, contains the popular Shaker tune "'Tis a Gift to Be Simple," and the second, *Rodeo*, has a famous "Hoe-Down."

The American West.

Musical nationalism created so much interest in ethnic music that some composers imported foreign styles from other countries into their own music, a practice that became known as **exoticism**. Examples of musical exoticism include Mendelssohn's "Scottish" and "Italian" symphonies, Tchaikovsky's *Capriccio Italien*, Rimsky-Korsakov's *Capriccio Espagnol*, and Dvořák's "American" string quartet and Symphony No. 9, "From the New World."

Exercise 24.1. Short Essay: Nationalist Composers

Select a nationalist composer from above and write a short essay that answers the following questions: When and where did the composer live throughout his life? How did he make a living? In what forms of composition did this person excel (operas, symphonies, concertos)? And what musical contributions did this composer make to the world of music?

LESSON 24.2

Peter Ilyich Tchaikovsky

Peter Ilyich Tchaikovsky (1840–1893) was a Russian composer who expertly balanced European musical traditions and Russian nationalist ideals in his works. He is best known for his concert overtures, his piano and violin concertos, his last three symphonies, and two of the world's most popular ballets: *The Nutcracker* and *Swan Lake*.

At the age of twenty, Tchaikovsky took music classes at the Russian Musical Society (RMS), where he met and formed lifelong relationships with a group of Russian nationalist composers—Balakirev, Rimsky-Korsakov, Borodin, Cui, and Mussorgsky—now known as the Mighty Five. The RMS encouraged local composers like Tchaikovsky to write music that used Russian folk songs and scales.

When he was twenty-two, Tchaikovsky enrolled at the new Saint Petersburg Conservatory, where he studied traditional European harmony and counterpoint and was exposed to all kinds of non-Russian music. Even though the RMS did not approve of the teachings at the Conservatory, Tchaikovsky managed to keep a good relationship with the Mighty Five and his Conservatory professors. He did not fully subscribe to the teachings of either school and instead worked to create a new style of music that combined the best of both European and Russian characteristics.

After graduating, Tchaikovsky got a job at the Moscow Conservatory, where he composed and taught music theory. He also worked as a music critic, which gave him the opportunity to travel abroad and hear the works of non-Russian composers like **Beethoven,** Brahms, and Schumann. During his years at the Moscow Conservatory, Tchaikovsky wrote his first successful work, a concert overture called *Romeo and Juliet*. He also wrote his second and third symphonies, his first piano concerto, the ballet *Swan Lake*, and a Slavic concert overture called *Marche Slave*.

In 1877, Tchaikovsky married a former student, but left her after a disastrous two-and-a-half months. Tchaikovsky fell into a depression and spent the next five years traveling alone throughout Europe and Russia, avoiding social contact whenever possible. During this difficult time, Tchaikovsky finished his Fourth Symphony, a violin concerto, the *Serenade for Strings*, and two concert overtures: *Capriccio Italien* and his *1812 Overture*. This last work was a nationalist programmatic piece written to commemorate Russia's defense against Napoleon's army. The score calls for real cannon fire depicting the fight against Napoleon, whose armies are musically conveyed by the French national anthem called *La Marseillaise*.

Through his travels Tchaikovsky became quite famous, and in 1884 the Russian Tsar Alexander III awarded him a title of nobility, which came with a lifetime annual salary. This very public show of approval helped the composer come out of his depression and re-enter public life. He finally settled back down in Russia, and in the last nine years of his life Tchaikovsky wrote his Fifth Symphony and his last two ballets: *The Sleeping Beauty* and *The Nutcracker*. In October of 1893, Tchaikovsky conducted the premiere of his Sixth Symphony ("Pathétique") in Saint Petersburg, just nine days before his death.

Unit 24 Study Guide

On a separate piece of paper, answer the following questions:

1. Describe musical nationalism and explain how it influenced orchestra music in the Romantic era. Include a few composers and compositions in your answer.
2. What is musical exoticism, and how is it different from musical nationalism?
3. Describe the main contributions that Tchaikovsky made to the world of orchestra music.

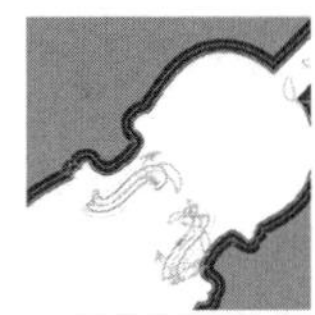

Unit 25. Minor Key Signatures

LESSON 25.1

Relative Minor

So far we have studied major key signatures and scales built on two major tetrachords. After major scales, the next most common scale found in orchestra music is the **minor scale**. Every minor scale shares a special relationship with one major scale.

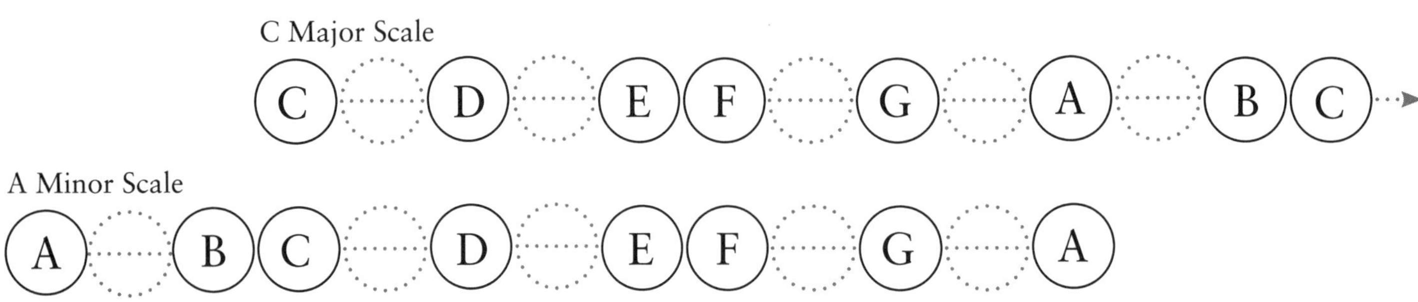

Above you will see that the scales of C major and A minor share the same notes, which means they also share the same key signature. The biggest difference between these two scales is the resting tone; that is, C major melodies usually end on the resting tone C, and A minor melodies end on A, which is the resting tone of the A minor scale.

Scales that share the same notes and key signatures are called "relatives." C major is the **relative major** of A minor, and A minor is the **relative minor** of C major. The first scale degree of the relative minor is always the sixth scale degree of the major scale, as shown below.

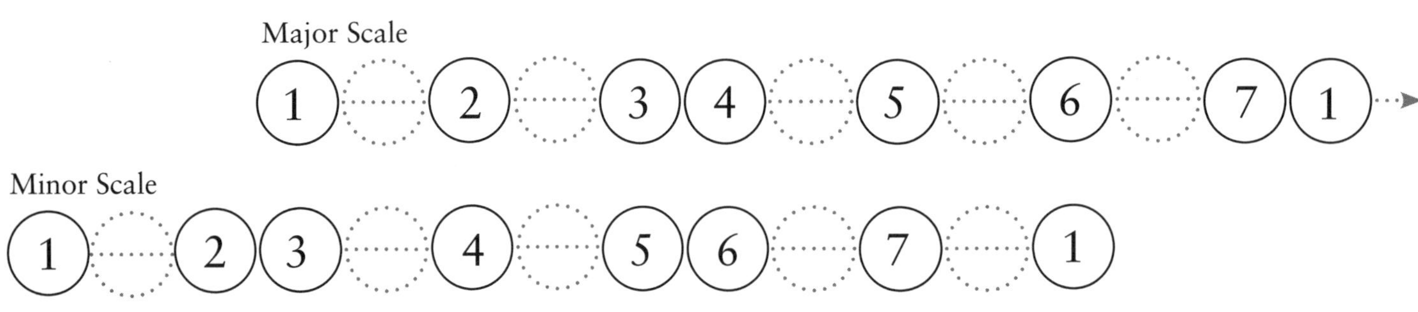

In the examples below, the whole note is on the resting tone of the major key, and the quarter note notehead is on the resting tone of the minor key. Instead of going up six scale degrees to find the relative minor key, it is easier to go down a minor third from the resting tone of the major key.

Exercise 25.1. Relative Minor

1. To figure out the relative minor, find the __________ scale degree of the major scale.
2. To determine the relative major, find the __________ scale degree of the minor scale.
3. Explain the biggest difference between a relative major and minor scale.________________________________

____

4. On the staves below, write a whole note on the resting tone for the major key, and write a filled in notehead on resting tone for the relative minor. The first one has been done for you.

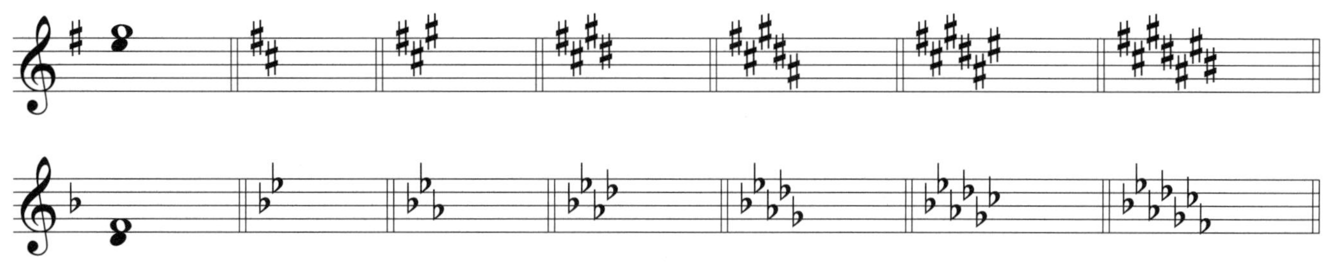

LESSON 25.2

Parallel Minor

Relative majors and minors share the same key signature but have a different resting tone. **Parallel majors and minors** share the same resting tone but have different key signatures. For example, the parallel minor of D major is D minor, and the parallel major to E minor is E major.

The key signature for the parallel minor has three more flats than its major counterpart. C major, for example, has zero flats, so C minor has three flats. F major has one flat, so F minor has four.

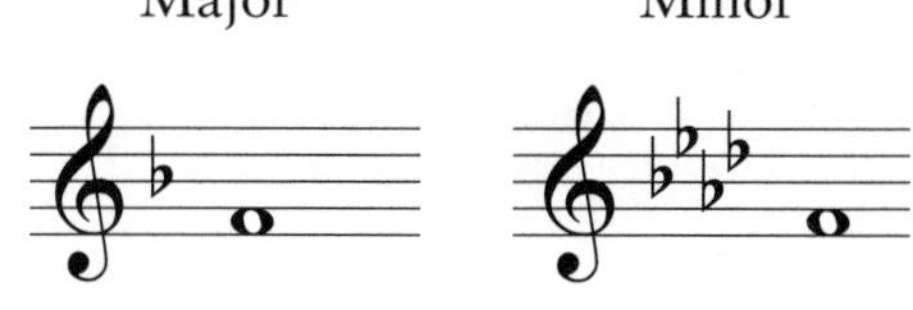

- In sharp keys, subtract three sharps. The key of E major has four sharps, so E minor has just one. The key of A major has three sharps, so A minor has none.
- If you run out of sharps to subtract, start adding flats. For example, G major has one sharp, so to add three flats, one must take away the one sharp from the G major key signature and add two more flats. G minor has two flats.

Exercise 25.2. Parallel Minor

1. Write the following major and minor key signatures on the staff below.

A Major	B Major	C Major	D Major	E Major	F Major	G Major
A Minor	B Minor	C Minor	D Minor	E Minor	F Minor	G Minor

LESSON 25.3

Major vs. Minor Melodies

Most melodies end on their resting tone, so the best way to determine if a melody is major or minor is to look at the last note of the melody. In the example below, the key signature has no sharps or flats, which means the key is either C major or A minor. The last note of the melody is A, so the melody is likely in the key of A minor.

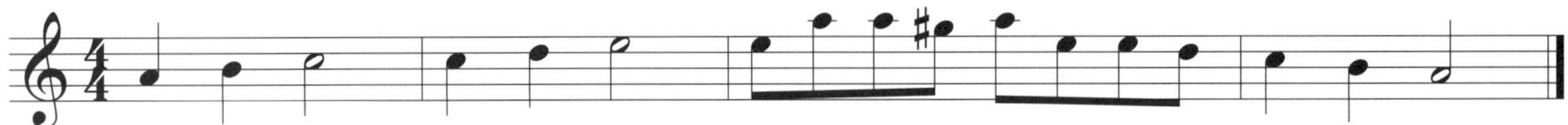

Exercise 25.3. Is the Melody Major or Minor?

When answering the questions below, include the term major or minor when describing a key.

1. The key signature is _____ major or _____ minor, and the last note of the melody is _____. So the melody is likely in the key of ________________________________.

2. The key signature is _____ major or _____ minor, and the last note of the melody is _____. So the melody is likely in the key of ________________________________.

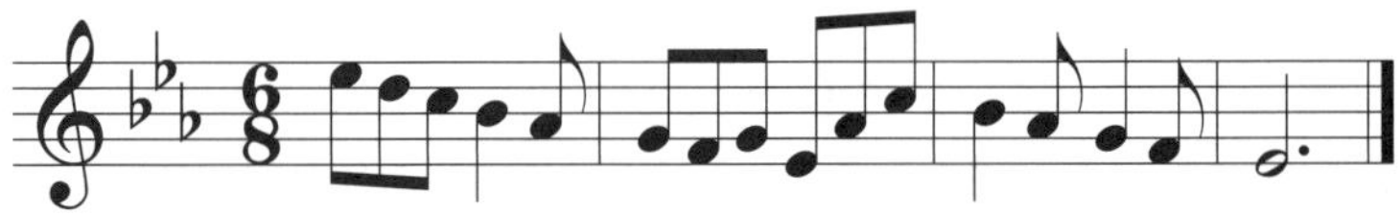

3. The key signature is _____ major or _____ minor, and the last note of the melody is _____. So the melody is likely in the key of ________________________________.

4. Using the same process from the questions above, you can figure out that this melody is likely in the key of _______________.

Unit 25 Study Guide

Complete the circle of fifths diagram on the next page. Then on a separate piece of paper, complete the following tasks:

1. Explain how to figure out the relative minor of a major key, and the relative major of a minor key.
2. Explain how to determine if a melody is major or minor.
3. Explain the difference between relative minor and parallel minor.
4. Explain how to figure out a minor key signature.
5. On a separate piece of staff paper, write your clef and the key signature for the relative minor and parallel minor of the following major keys: A, B, C, D, E, F, and G major.

The Circle of Fifths

1. First, write your clef on each staff. Then write the key signature with the number of sharps or flats specified for each key. The keys with one flat, zero flats or sharps, and one sharp have been done for you.
2. In the blank space above each staff, write the newest sharp or flat note in each key signature. In the key of F, the newest flat is B♭, as shown. In the key of G, for example, the newest sharp is F♯.
3. In the outermost circle that is shaded gray, write the letter name of the major key in UPPERCASE letters. The keys of F major, C major, and G major have already been done for you. Toward the bottom of the diagram, you will notice there are dotted lines that divide the spaces in half. Those keys have two enharmonic names—one sharp name and one flat name.
4. In the inner circle, write the letter name of the relative minor key in lowercase letters. The keys of D minor, A minor, and E minor have already been done for you.

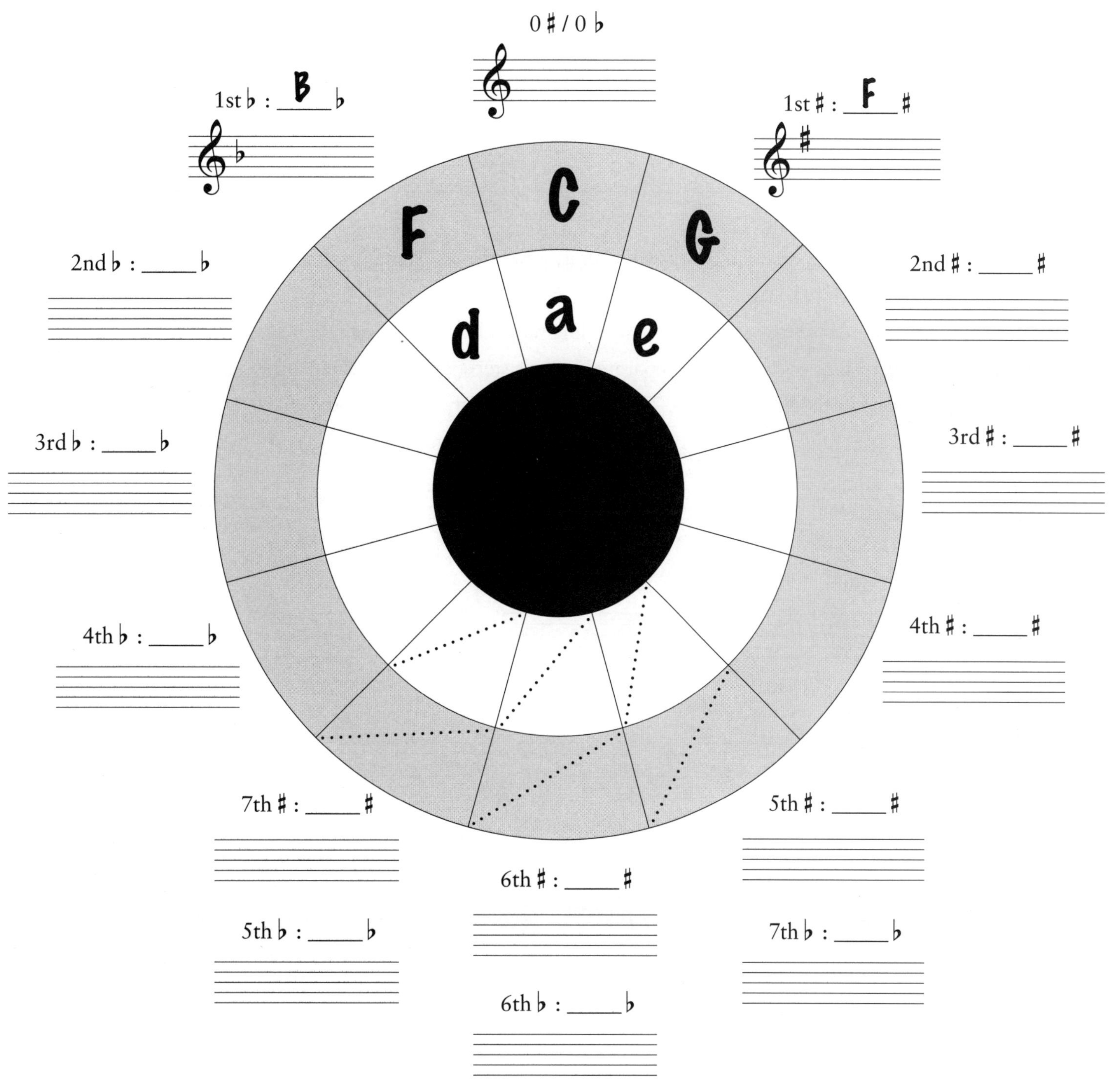

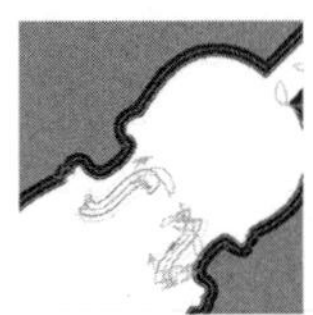

Unit 26. Minor Scales

LESSON 26.1

Natural Minor Scales

In this unit we will study three types of minor scales: natural minor, harmonic minor, and melodic minor. **Natural minor scales** only use notes that exist within the key signature. The key signature for C minor has three flats, so the C natural minor scale only uses the notes from that key, as shown below. All natural minor scales have half steps between scale degrees 2 and 3, and between 5 and 6.

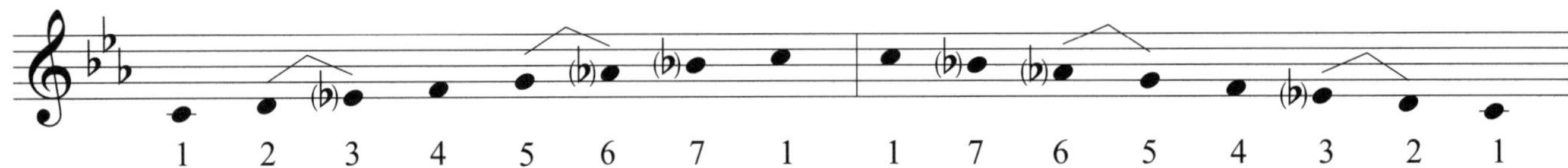

Exercise 26.1. Natural Minor Scales

1. Using the strategies you learned in the previous unit, write the key signature for the minor key identified at the beginning of each staff.
2. Then write the one-octave ascending and descending natural minor scale that corresponds to that key.
3. Write half step markings over the notes separated by half steps, and write accidentals next to the notes that have sharps or flats in the key signature. The first one has been done for you.

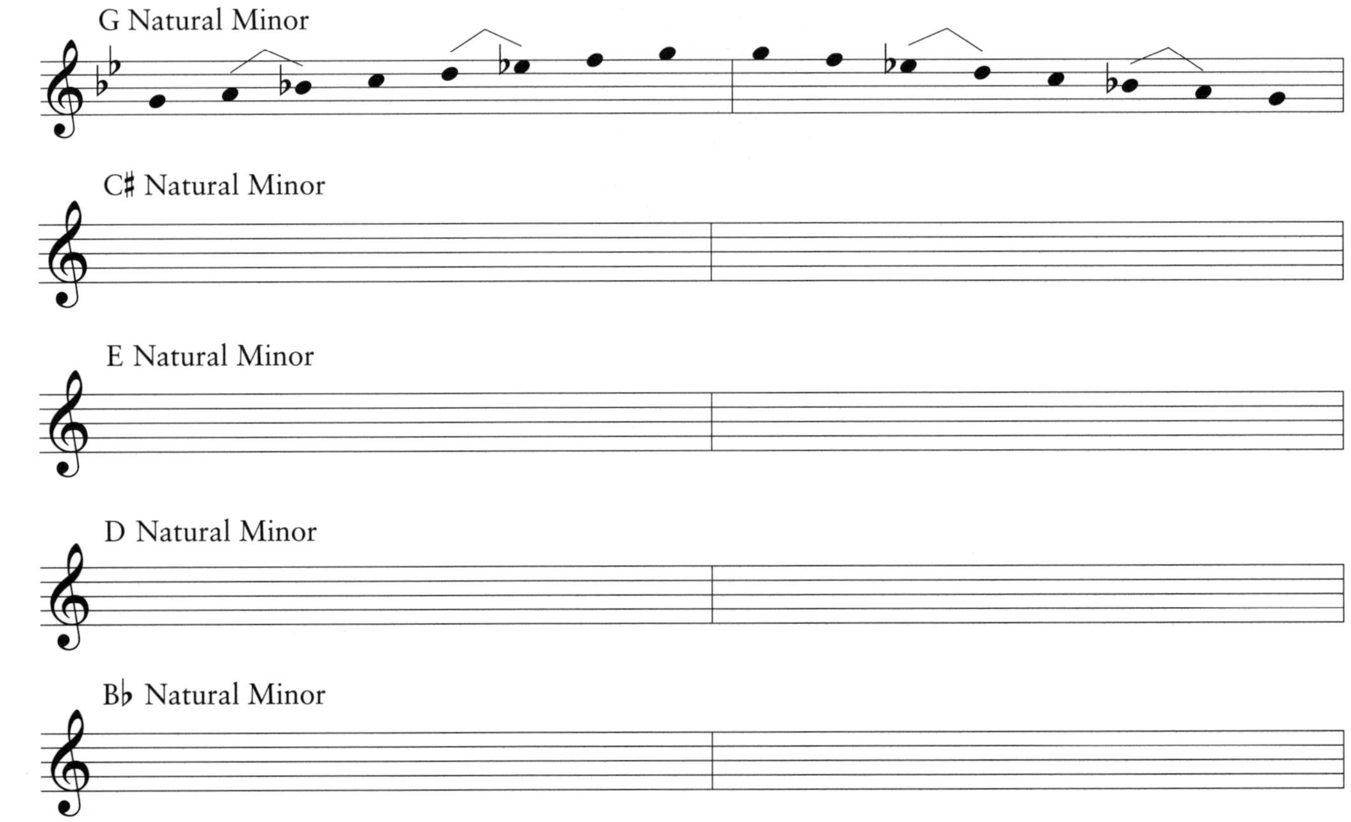

LESSON 26.2

The Difference Between Major and Minor Scales

Compare the major and natural minor scales below. The notes are similar except for the third, sixth, and seventh scale degrees. In major scales these three scale degrees are "raised," and in minor scales they are "lowered." This is true for all major and natural minor scales.

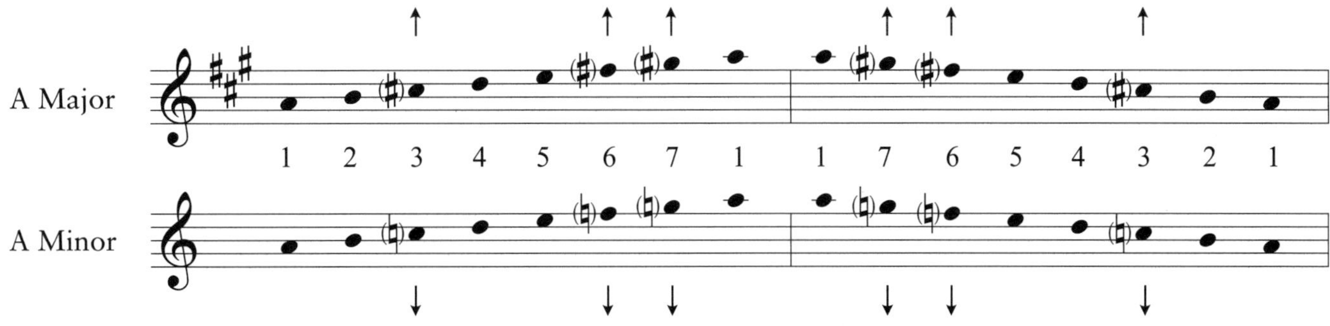

In major scales, the distances from the resting tone to the third, sixth, and seventh scale degrees are a major third, major sixth, and major seventh, respectively.

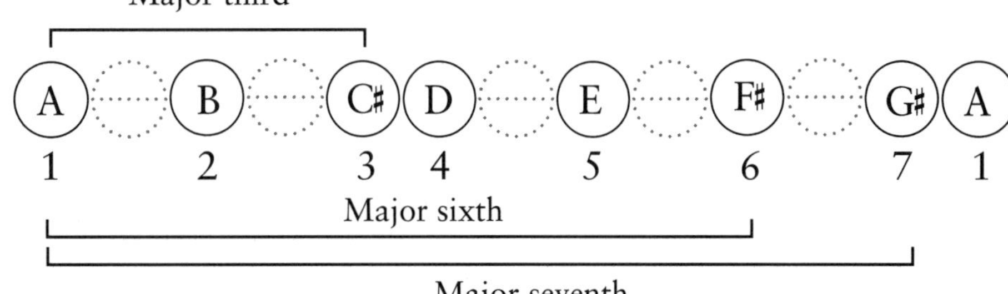

In minor scales, the distances from the resting tone to the same scale degrees are a minor third, minor sixth, and minor seventh, respectively.

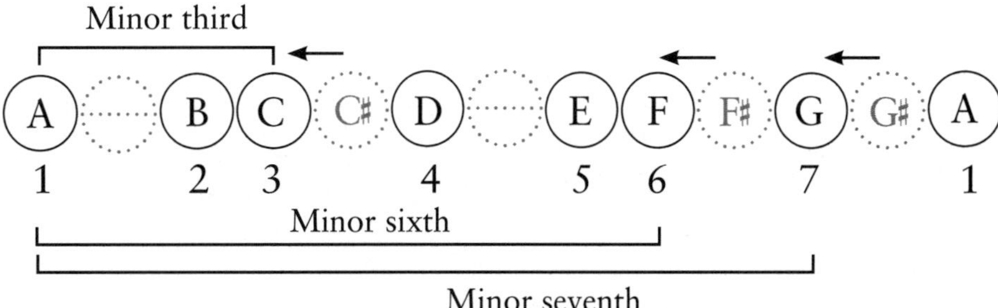

Exercise 26.2. The Difference Between Major and Minor Scales

1. Change the following major scales to minor by adding accidentals to lower the third, sixth, and seventh scale degrees. Look closely at the major key signatures and use a natural to lower a sharp note, or a flat to lower a natural note. Then write half step marks over the notes separated by half steps like in the example.

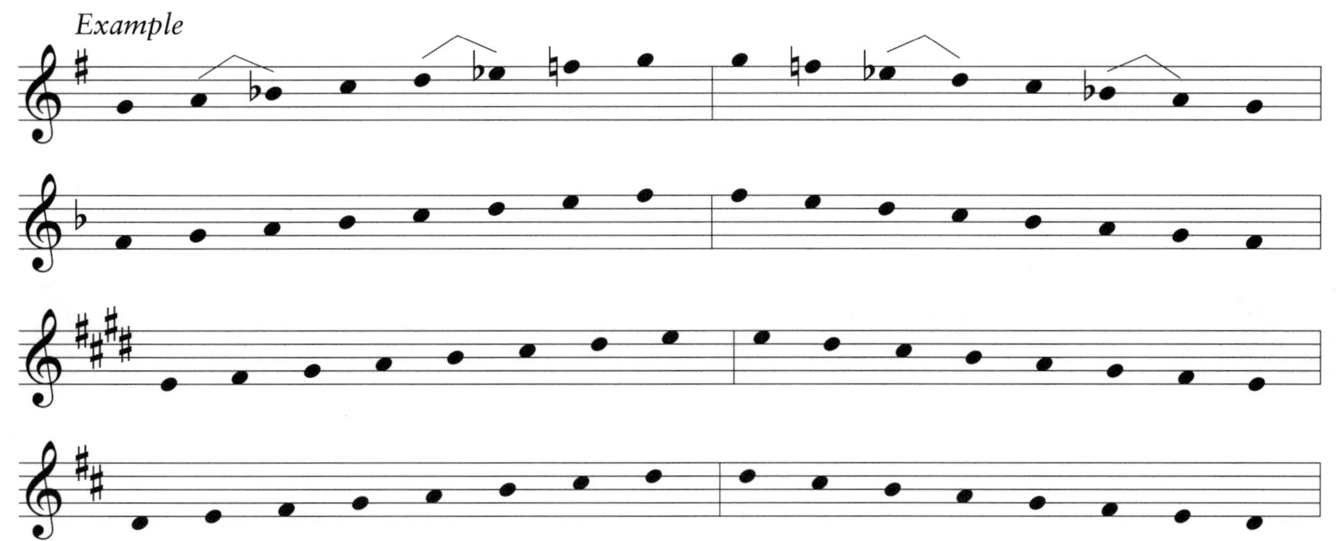

LESSON 26.3

Harmonic Minor Scales

The third scale degree is *always* lowered in all forms of minor scales; the minor third between the resting tone and the third scale degree never changes. In the natural minor scales studied in the previous lesson, the sixth and seventh scale degrees are also always lowered and never raised. In **harmonic minor scales**, the sixth remains lowered, but the seventh scale degree is raised a half step, as shown below. The raised seventh creates a third half step in the scale (between scale degrees 7 and 1) and an augmented second between the sixth and seventh scale degrees. An **augmented second** is a type of second with a distance of three half steps, as shown below.

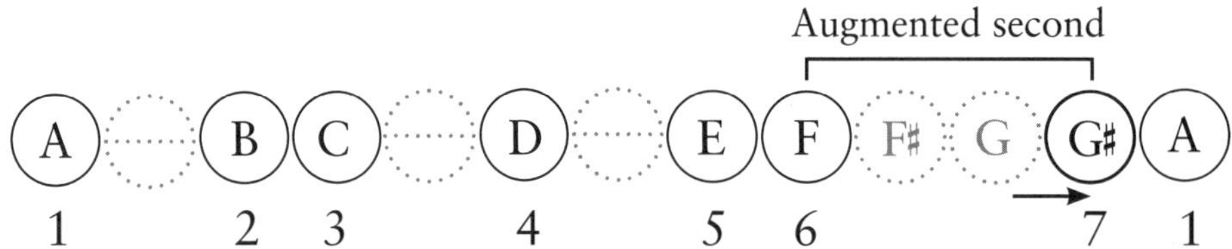

Even though this interval is the same distance as a minor third, it is *not* a third. In the A harmonic minor scale above, the interval between F and G♯ must be some kind of second because the note names are sequential. In the C harmonic minor scale below, the augmented second looks like a second, not a third. To raise the seventh scale degree, a sharp sign is used when the note is natural, and a natural sign is used to raise flat notes, as shown below.

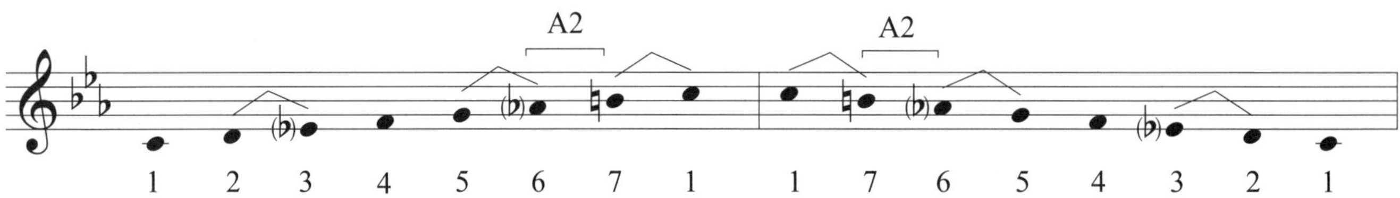

Exercise 26.3. Harmonic Minor Scales

1. Write the key signature for the minor key identified at the beginning of each staff.
2. Then write a one-octave ascending and descending harmonic minor scale using the correct accidental to raise the seventh scale degree.
3. Finally, write half step markings over the three pairs of half steps, and write "A2" above the augmented second, like in the C harmonic minor scale written above.

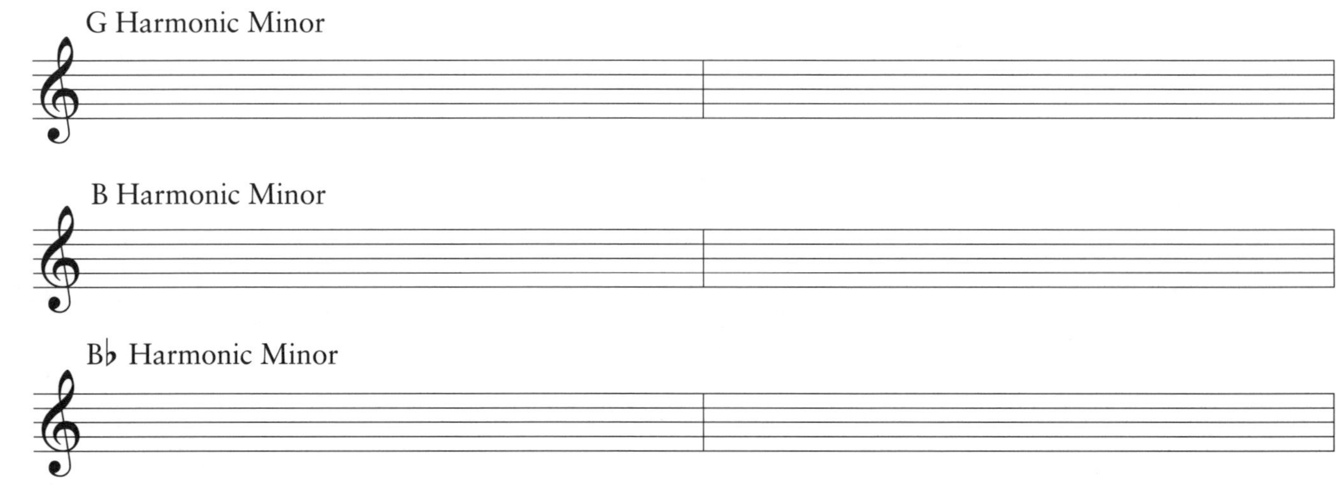

LESSON 26.4

Melodic Minor Scales

The augmented second is an awkwardly wide interval in a melody. To get around this problem, composers use the **melodic minor scale** for melodic passages. In melodic minor scales the sixth and seventh scale degrees are both raised when ascending up the scale, and both scale degrees are lowered to their natural minor form when descending. Notice the difference between the ascending and descending D melodic minor scale below; the half steps are in different places in the ascending and descending scales, and there are no augmented seconds.

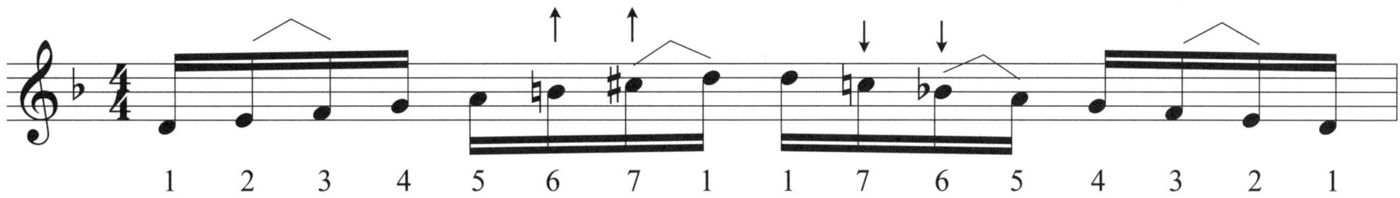

Exercise 26.4. Melodic Minor Scales

1. On the staves below, write the key signature and ascending/descending melodic minor scales in the given keys. Use sixteenth notes like the D melodic minor scale directly above.

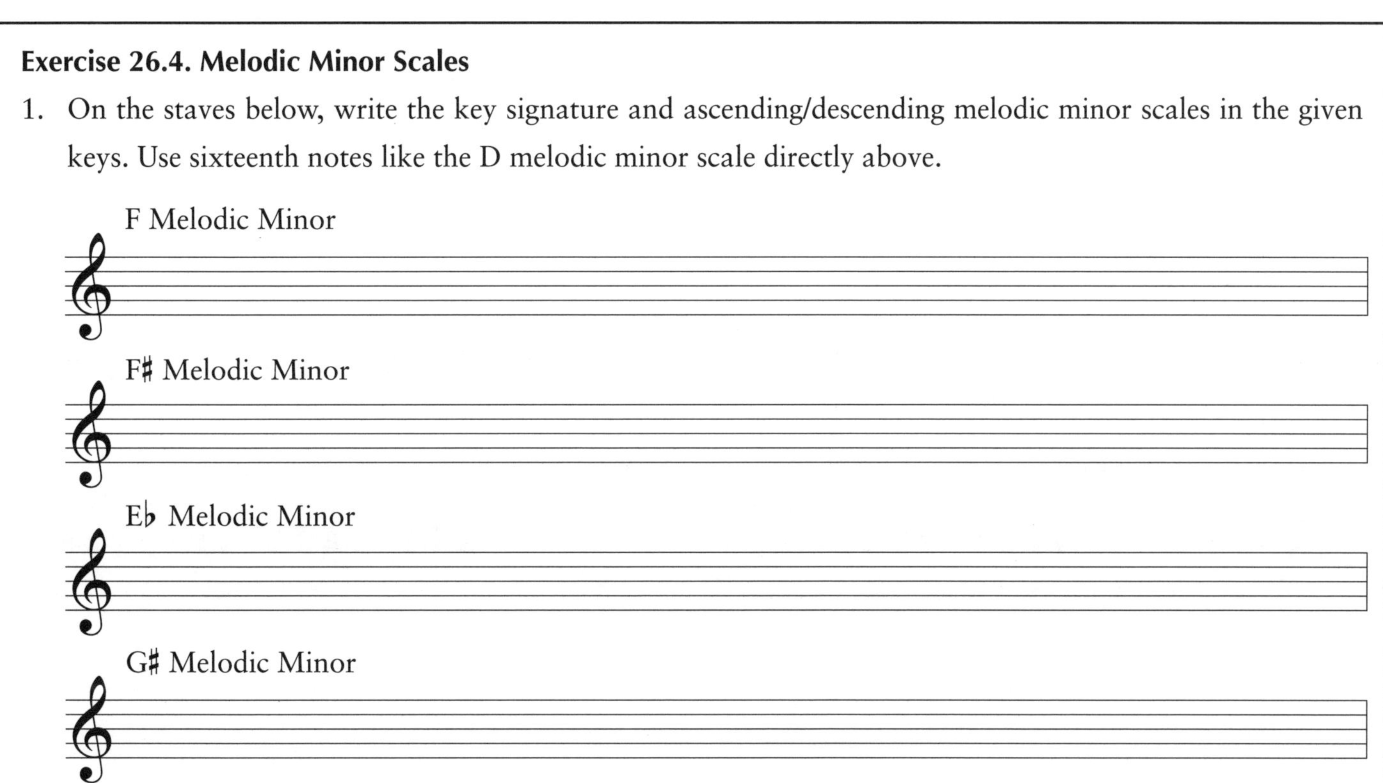

Unit 26 Study Guide

On a separate piece of paper, answer the following questions:

1. What is the difference between relative minor and parallel minor? Give examples.
2. Explain the difference between natural, harmonic, and melodic minor in terms of scale degrees.
3. What is an augmented second? How is it similar to and different from a minor third?
4. Explain the difference between major and minor scales in terms of thirds, sixths, and sevenths.

On a separate piece of staff paper, complete the following tasks:

5. Write your clef and all key signatures from five sharps to five flats with one key signature on each staff.
6. Write a one-octave ascending and descending harmonic minor scale and a one-octave ascending and descending melodic minor scale that agrees with the key signature on each staff.
7. Add half step markings to your scales and write "A2" over any augmented seconds.

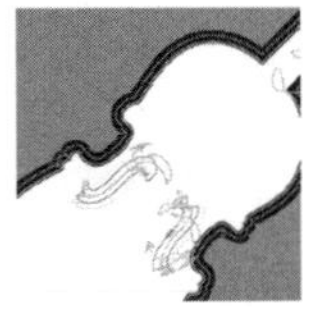

Unit 27. Jam Session

Few things in music are more fun than being part of a good jam session with your friends. Get in a group of three or more players and take turns playing the different parts of the chord progression here. The biggest/lowest instrument usually plays the bottom notes, known as the bass line, and the smaller instruments play the upper notes.

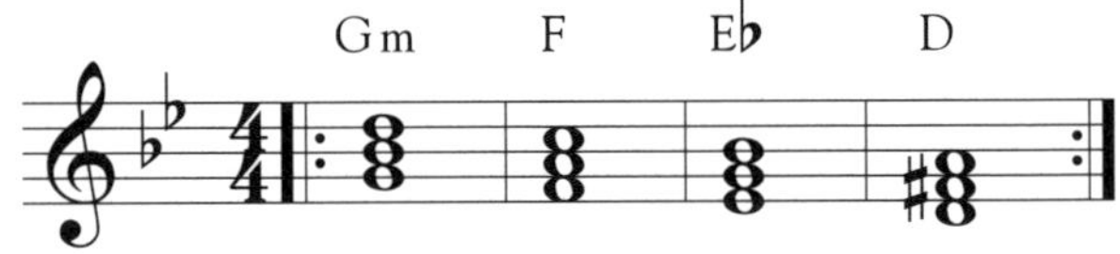

Rhythm

Add rhythms to your chord progression. Experiment with placing accents on beats 2 and 4. Try out the different rhythmic examples below, or create your own.

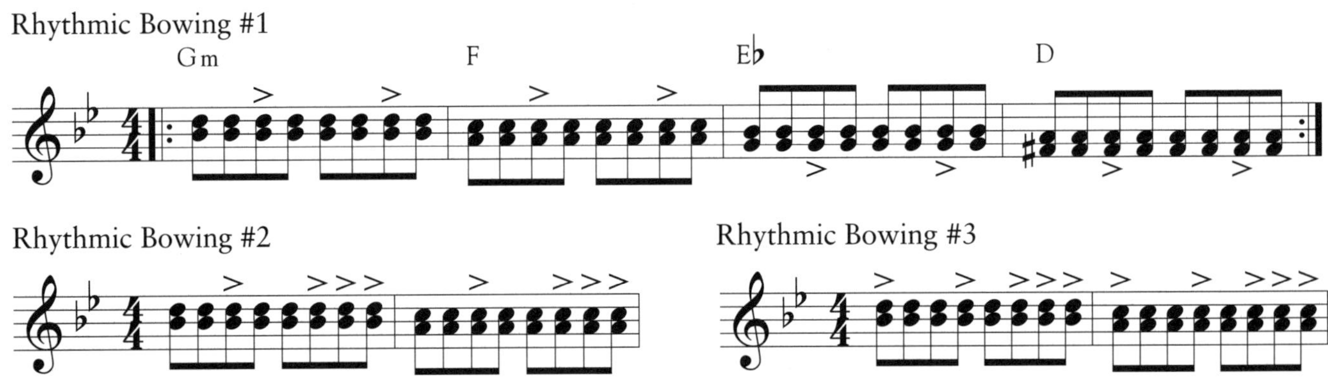

Swing or no swing? Remember, eighth notes can be played evenly or unevenly, with the first note of each pair longer than the second. This is called "swing."

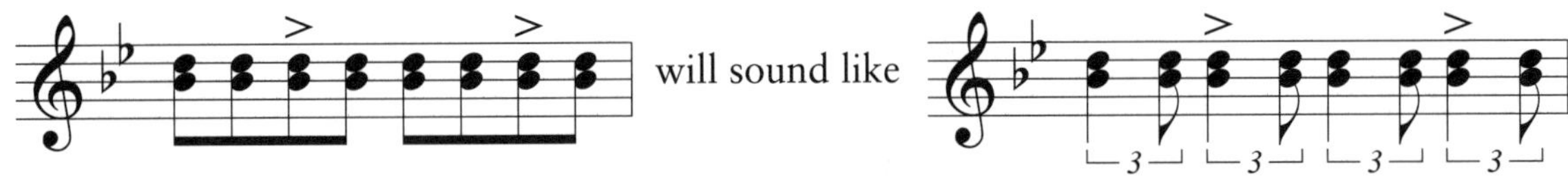

You can create more emphasis on beats 2 and 4 by adding chops or chords, as shown below. Chops are performed by "crunching" the bow against the string while holding the strings lightly with the left hand so they don't ring. The best way to learn how to chop is to find someone who can teach you, or look it up on YouTube. Playing chops takes practice; it is not as easy as it looks.

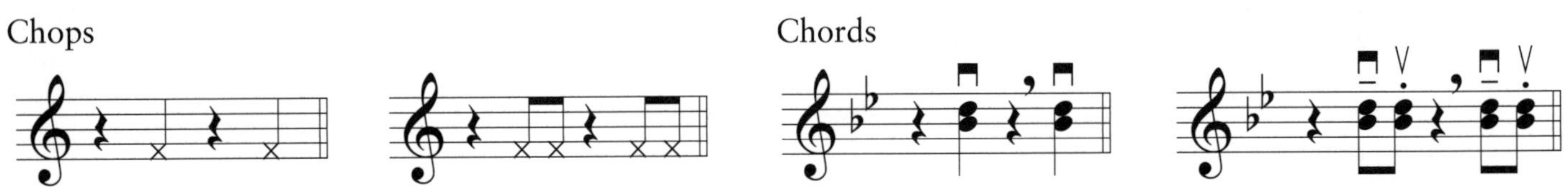

Bass Line and Melody

The bass line is the lowest and most important line of notes in a chord progression. It can be played with long tones, such as whole notes, or with a driving rhythm that sets the character of the piece. The bass line usually starts on the bottom note of the chord each time the chord changes, but it may include other notes between the chord changes. Try out the examples below, or create your own.

The melody is the most important musical line above the bass line. It is usually written or improvised in the upper range of the instrument where it can be heard above the chords. When creating a melody, keep it simple and use mostly chord tones until you get more comfortable adding non-chord tones. Try improvising over the progression at the top of page 48, or use one of the four progressions below.

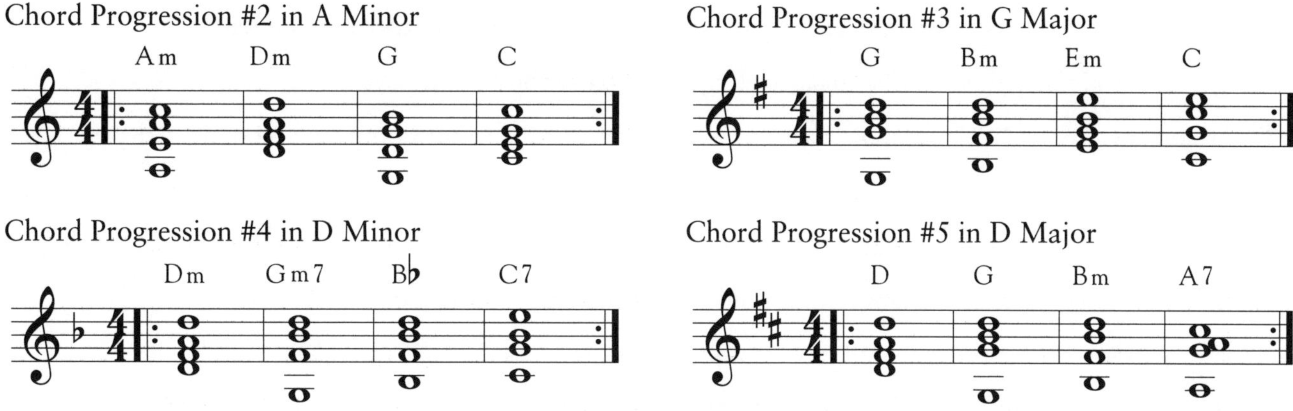

Unit 27 Final Project

Get in a group of three to five players with diverse instrumentation and create a piece using one of the chord progressions from this unit. Create a plan for how your piece will begin, develop, and end. Use the model outlined below or create your own. Rehearse your piece, and then play it for your teacher (or the class).

1. Introduction: How are you going to begin? Soft or loud? With everyone or just one person? Start simply with a whole note chord progression or maybe with a pizzicato bass line.
2. Rhythm Plan: Start simply with chops and then add chords and rhythmic bowing as the piece develops.
3. Melody: Create or **improvise** a melody while others back up the soloist with rhythmic harmonies and bass line. Decide the order of the soloists who will improvise.
4. Grand Finale: Take the melody up an octave and add plenty of embellishment. Accompany with *forte* eighth notes, chords, and a strong bass line. Then fade out or end together on one of the chords.

Glossary

augmented second. A type of second that has three half steps between the two notes, commonly seen in harmonic minor scales. (p. 46)

Bach, Johann Sebastian (1685–1750). German composer of the Baroque era whose use of counterpoint, harmony, and fugue served as a model for many of the great composers who followed him. His most popular works for strings include his six *Brandenburg Concertos*, his violin concertos, and his unaccompanied suites for cello and violin. (p. 14)

ballet. A form of carefully choreographed dance characterized by a refined repertoire of light, graceful movements that originated from the courtly dances of the Italian Renaissance. (p. 38)

Baroque era. The musical period between 1600 and 1750 that includes composers such as Corelli, Vivaldi, J.S. Bach, Handel, and Lully. (p. 14)

Beethoven, Ludwig van (1770–1827). German composer who bridged the Classical and Romantic eras. (p. 39)

chromatic. A term applied to a scale or part of a scale that is made up of half steps. (p. 6)

Classical era. The musical period between 1730 and 1820 that includes composers such as J.C. Bach, C.P.E. Bach, Stamitz, Haydn, Mozart, and Beethoven. (p. 25)

compound meter. Music with beats that are divided into three equal parts, most often with dotted quarter note beats that are divided into three eighth notes. (p. 20)

concerto. A piece for solo instrument(s) accompanied by orchestra, often in three movements. (p. 25)

concerto grosso. A piece with several soloists accompanied by orchestra. (p. 15)

Corelli, Arcangelo (1653–1713). Italian Baroque era violin virtuoso and composer who helped popularize the violin sonata and concerto grosso. (p. 14)

détaché. Detached. A bowing term that indicates the music is bowed "as it comes" and not slurred. (p. 24)

dotted rhythm. A dot increases the length of a note or rest by half of its value. (p. 12)

duple meter. Music with beats organized into groups of two, such as $\frac{2}{4}$ or $\frac{4}{4}$. (p. 9, 20)

enharmonic. Two notes that sound the same but are written differently, such as A♯ and B♭. (p. 5)

exoticism. A compositional practice common among nationalist composers during the Romantic era in which they imported musical characteristics from other countries into their own music. (p. 38)

half step. The smallest interval in string music; two notes separated by a half step have no notes between them. (p. 5)

Handel, George Frideric (1685–1759). German-born Baroque era composer who settled in London and was known for his oratorios, operas, and keyboard concertos. His most popular works with strings include the oratorio *Messiah* and his two orchestral suites: *Water Music* and *Music for the Royal Fireworks*. (p. 15)

harmonic minor scale. A form of the minor scale that has a lowered sixth scale degree and a raised seventh scale degree. (p. 46)

Haydn, Franz Joseph (1732–1809). Austrian composer of the Classical era who developed and popularized the piano trio, string quartet, and the symphony. (p. 25)

improvise. To create and perform music in the moment without a score and not from memory. (p. 49)

interval. The distance between two notes, often measured in terms of half and whole steps. (p. 7)

key signature. A group of sharps or flats after the clef that indicates which notes on the staff should be performed sharp or flat. (p. 28)

major. Big; bigger. Usually describes an interval that is one half step bigger than the minor interval of the same name. (p. 7)

major scale. A scale made up of two major tetrachords separated by a major second. In a major scale, the distances from the resting tone to the third, sixth, and seventh scale degrees are a major third, major sixth, and major seventh, respectively. (p. 26)

melodic minor scale. A form of minor scale in which the sixth and seventh scale degrees are raised when ascending and lowered when descending. (p. 47)

meter. Describes how the beats in a piece of music are grouped and divided. (p. 9)

minor. Small; smaller. Usually describes an interval that is one half step smaller than the major interval of the same name. (p. 7)

minor scale. A scale in which the distance from the resting tone to the third scale degree is a minor third; the distance to the sixth and seventh scale degrees varies depending on the type of minor scale—natural, harmonic, or melodic minor. (p. 40)

Mozart, Wolfgang Amadeus (1756–1791). Classical era composer whose ability to write moving, sophisticated melodies naturally contributed advancements to both opera and the concerto. (p. 25)

nationalism. A sentiment of national loyalty and identity that appeared in music and other art forms during the Romantic era. (p. 38)

natural. A term used to describe a note that is neither flat nor sharp. When used as an accidental, the symbol (♮) cancels a flat or sharp sign. (p. 5)

natural minor scale. A form of minor scale that only use notes within the key signature and no other chromatic notes. (p. 44)

opera. A staged drama in which most of the lines are sung and singers are accompanied by an orchestra. (p. 14)

oratorio. A work for choir and orchestra that tells a story, often a Biblical story, with text sung by soloists and choir. Unlike opera, oratorios do not have acting, staging, or costumes. (p. 14)

parallel major/minor. Two keys that share the same resting tone but have different key signatures. (p. 41)

relative major/minor. Two keys that share the same key signature but have different resting tones. (p. 40)

Renaissance. French for "rebirth," this term refers to the musical period between 1400 and 1600 during which many inventors, artists, and writers began making significant scientific and philosophical advancements that brought the world into the modern era. (p. 14)

Romantic era. The musical period between 1800 and 1910 that includes composers such as Beethoven, Schubert, Mendelssohn, Tchaikovsky, Brahms, Dvořák, Rimsky-Korsakov, and Strauss. (p. 38)

sautillé. Springing. A bowing term that is associated with sixteenth notes that are performed near the balance point in such a way that the bow naturally begins to bounce, creating a crisp, detached articulation. (p. 24)

scale degree. A number that identifies the note's placement within the order of the scale. For example, the fourth scale degree is the fourth note of the scale. (p. 27)

second. An interval with two notes that are right next to each other on the staff, such as A to B and D to C. A minor second is one half step, and a major second is two half steps. (p. 7)

simple meter. Music with beats that are divided into two equal parts, most often with quarter note beats that are divided into two eighth notes. (p. 20)

sonata. Originally a work that was performed on an instrument instead of sung. Today the term refers to a work for piano or for solo instrument and piano, often in three movements. (p. 14)

spiccato. A bow stroke common in Classical era music in which the bow is bounced off the string. (p. 24)

string quartet. A work for two violins, viola, and cello that became popular during the Classical era. The term also refers to a chamber ensemble made up of two violins, viola, and a cello. (p. 25)

suite. A collection of dance movements combined into a single work, usually introduced by a one-movement prelude or overture. (p. 14)

sul ponticello. A bowing term that directs the performer to bow next to the bridge, creating a metallic tone. (p. 24)

sul tasto. A bowing term that directs the performer to bow over the fingerboard, creating an airy tone. (p. 24)

symphony. A musical work for orchestra, most often in four movements, that originated in the Classical era. The term also refers to a musical ensemble with sections of string instruments including first violins, second violins, viola, cello, and bass, as well as woodwinds, brass, and percussion. (p. 25)

syncopation. A compositional device in which the off beat notes are accentuated and tied over the beat, effectively hiding the beat with rests or ties. (p. 12)

Tchaikovsky, Peter Ilyich (1840–1893). A Romantic era Russian composer who balanced European and Russian nationalist musical ideals in his works. (p. 39)

tetrachord. A group of four consecutive notes separated by major and minor seconds. The four most common tetrachords include the major, minor, Phrygian, and Lydian tetrachords found on page 17. (p. 16)

third. A two-note interval that skips a note on the staff, such as A to C or G to B. A minor third is one-and-a-half whole steps, and a major third is two whole steps. (p. 18)

time signature. A fraction-like symbol that indicates how beats are organized in each measure. (p. 9)

Tourte, François (1747–1835). French bow maker who standardized the length, weight, size, and shape of the bow design we still use today. (p. 24)

triple meter. Music with beats organized into groups of three, such as $\frac{3}{4}$ or $\frac{3}{2}$. (p. 9, 20)

triplet. A beat of duple meter that is divided into three equal parts and indicated by the number 3 written over the notes. (p. 37)

Vivaldi, Antonio (1678–1741). Italian Baroque composer who wrote over five hundred concertos mostly for his students at a Venetian orphanage called the Ospedale della Pietà. (p. 14)